In the Steps of the Master

By
Dr. Joe Arthur

SWORD of the LORD
PUBLISHERS

Post Office Box 1099 • Murfreesboro, Tennessee 37133

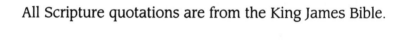

All Scripture quotations are from the King James Bible.

Contents

Foreword

When a fire burns, you can see it. You can feel the heat, and you can smell the smoke. Even so, when a fire burns in a man's heart, it cannot be hidden from the rest of us. That 'fire in my bones' (Jer. 20:9) is what we see when the fire of God is ablaze in the man declaring the message.

Dr. Joe Arthur is a man in whom the fire burns. If you talk with him, you sense it. If you hear him in front of an audience, you know it. Now in the pages of *In the Steps of the Master,* it is just as real.

As you walk your way through the Gospels with Dr. Arthur, you'll be blessed with each step you take. You'll learn the historic details. You'll understand the great truths. You'll grasp the heavenly mandates. You'll draw close to the Saviour.

If you are hurting, *In the Steps of the Master* will bring you healing!

If you are in doubt, every page will build your faith!

If you are struggling, you will be comforted!

If you are living in carnality, you will be motivated to move onto holy ground!

If you are uncertain about the will of God, you will likely get your bearings.

If you are lacking joy, you are going to be encouraged.

If you are unfruitful in your witness, you are going to be strengthened.

In a word, there's a very real possibility that a fire will begin to burn in you as you make your way in the steps of the Master.

Dr. Shelton Smith

Introduction

As we approach this subject, we must realize that we are studying the life of the greatest Man who ever has lived or ever will live. That is why the Song of Solomon says, speaking of our Lord, "[He] is...the chiefest among ten thousand....he is altogether lovely" (Song of Sol. 5:10,16). He is our Lord, our Saviour and our soon-coming King.

The Bible is the written Word of God. It is God's inspired, infallible, inerrant, indispensable Word. Thank God for His Holy Word that tells of His Son, Jesus. On the other hand, Jesus is the living Word of God, the Word of God in the flesh. In fact, one of the titles given to our Lord is "The Word of God" (Rev. 19:13). The Bible is God's Word in ink, and Jesus is God's Word in blood. The Bible is the inspired Word, but Jesus is the Incarnate Word.

One cannot separate Jesus from the Bible. Jesus is the very heart and life of the Bible. He is the central theme and melodious song of Scripture. If Jesus is taken out of the Bible, all that is left is a lifeless book on paper. Jesus is in every book, in every chapter and on every page.

The Bible has two main divisions, the Old Testament and the New Testament. Both of these divisions ring out the praises of Jesus. The Bible is the sharp two-edged Sword that came out of the mouth of the resurrected Christ whom John saw on the isle of Patmos (Rev. 1:16). Jesus is the Word of God in flesh given to show mankind the way to God, joy, peace and salvation.

In the Steps of the Master

The Old Testament contains one great message, and that message is, "Someone is coming!" We who are saved know that this "Someone" is Jesus Christ, our wonderful Lord. From Genesis to Malachi, the Old Testament is filled with types and foreshadowings of the coming Christ. Many times Jesus appears in the form of a theophany, an Old Testament appearance of Jesus Christ. Jesus is very real in the Old Testament.

When God tells Adam and Eve that the Seed of the woman will bruise the head of the serpent (Gen. 3:15), we receive a glimpse of Jesus. Passing by the smoking altar of Abel where he has offered the best lamb of his flock (4:4), we get a glimpse of Jesus. Approaching the Tabernacle on the Day of Atonement (Lev. 16), we get a glimpse of Jesus. When the sun shines off the brazen serpent in the wilderness (Num. 21:9), we get a glimpse of Jesus. When we hear the message of the prophets, we hear the message of Jesus. In the character of Joseph, the courage of David, the wisdom of Solomon, the power of Elijah, we get a glimpse of Jesus, the Son of God. Jesus Christ is the underlying theme of every book in the Old Testament. We can see His presence behind the scenes.

In Genesis, He is the Promised Seed. In Exodus, He is the Passover Lamb. In Leviticus, He is the Great High Priest. In Numbers, He is the Star out of Jacob. In Deuteronomy, He is the Prophet like unto Moses. In Joshua, He is the Captain of our salvation. In Judges, He is the Judge who judges in righteousness. In Ruth, He is our Kinsman Redeemer. In Samuel, He is the Anointed of God. In Kings, He is the Lord of Heaven. In Chronicles, He is the Great History Maker. In Ezra, He is the Ready Scribe and the Restorer of the temple. In Nehemiah, He is the Builder of the walls. In Esther, He is our Intercessor. In Job, He is the Horse of Power pawing in the valleys of life. In Psalms, He is the Song and the Shepherd of the sheep. In Proverbs, He is the Wisdom of God. In Ecclesiastes, He is the Great Preacher. In the Song of Solomon, He is the Great Lover of my soul, my Beloved, my Friend. In Isaiah, He is the suffering Servant of God. In Jeremiah, He is the Lord our Righteousness. In Lamentations, He is the Weeping Prophet. In Ezekiel, He is the One sitting on the throne. In Daniel, He is the Fourth Man in the fire. In Hosea, He is the One who loves the unlovely. In Joel, He is the Lord our Bounty. In Amos, He is the Rescuer of Israel. In Obadiah, He is the Deliverer on Mount Zion. In Jonah, He is the buried and risen Saviour. In Micah, He is the Everlasting God. In Nahum, He is our Stronghold in the day of wrath. In Habakkuk, He is our Anchor of Faith. In Zephaniah, He is our Judgment and Cleansing. In Haggai, He is the Smitten Shepherd. In Zechariah, He is a Fountain open for sin. In Malachi, He is the Sun of Righteousness who is going to arise with healing in His wings.

That Someone who is coming is Jesus, and after the close of the Old Testament and the four hundred years of silence, John the Baptist on the banks of the Jordan River points to that Someone and says, "Behold the Lamb of God, which taketh away the sin of the world" (John 1:29). The angels come out and say from the heavens, "He is here"; Simeon says, "He is here"; Anna says, "He is here"; then we hear Jesus say, "*I* am here."

As we follow the Master from His birth to His ascension, we will examine the life, ministry and, most of all, the love and salvation offered by our Lord. At the end of this book, only part of the half will have been told. When we look at the life of Christ, the way He loved, taught and worked miracles, we must say with all our hearts, "Truly He was, is and forevermore shall be the Son of God."

1

Subject: The Birth of Jesus Christ

Text: Matthew 1:18–25

I. It Was a Visioned Birth.
    A. Seen by Adam in Genesis 3:15
    B. Seen by Abraham in Isaac
    C. Seen by Isaiah in Isaiah 7 and 9
    D. Seen by Other Prophets
    E. Seen by Joseph in Matthew 1

II. It Was a Vital Birth.
    A. To Fulfill the Scripture (Heb. 7:11)
    B. To Provide the Saviour (Luke 2:11)
    C. To Bring Hope to a Lost Society (Luke 2:14)

III. It Was a Virgin Birth.
    A. The Purity of the Woman (Matt. 1:18)
    B. The Perfection of the Seed (Luke 1:35)
    C. The Performance of the Holy Spirit (Matt. 1:20)

IV. It Was a Victorious Birth.
    A. Over Satan (Gen. 3:15)
    B. Over Sin (Matt. 1:21)
    C. Over Society (Luke 1:32, 33)

The Birth of Jesus Christ

The birth of our Lord Jesus Christ is without a doubt one of the greatest events in the history of the world. No other single event has made as great an impact upon people's lives as His birth has. Not only was it a great event, but it was also one of the greatest miracles of the Bible. The birth of Jesus wrought such a change in the world that it affected even the way that we measure time. The years before Jesus came are now designated "B.C." (before Christ). The years following His birth are labeled "A.D." (anno Domini), which means "in the year of our Lord." Even the lost world must see that He is real.

Jesus never wrote a book, never bought a house, never took a really long trip and was never recognized by the kings; He was never accepted by the religious crowd of His day. Nevertheless, many books have been written about Him, He bought and built the greatest house the world has ever known, people have traveled millions of miles telling His story, and one day all the kings and religious leaders of all time will bow before the Son of God. No other person in the history of the human race has had more influence on the world and the people in it than this King who was born so long ago.

In the Steps of the Master

The birth of Jesus was foretold by God in Scripture. It was neither an accident nor an afterthought. This birth was planned by God before the foundation of the world.

The birth of Jesus was a visioned birth, seen in type and foreshadowed throughout the Old Testament. Through Adam and Eve, in the Garden of Eden, we get a glimpse of the coming of the promised Seed. Adam and Eve were told by God not to eat the fruit of the tree; but they fell, broke their fellowship with God and plunged the whole human race into sin and disobedience. Their eyes were opened, and they knew they had displeased God. In the cool of the day, God came into the Garden and reproved them for what they had done. He put a curse on the ground, causing it to grow thorns better than it grows flowers. He put a curse on the man. God also put a curse on the serpent, commanding it to crawl on its belly; along with that, He told the serpent that one day its head would be eternally bruised. Then God put a curse on the woman; God said that in sorrow she would give birth to children, thereby causing childbirth to be painful.

However, in the midst of all the curses and calamity, God let the light of His love and grace shine through. He made a proclamation stating that the Seed of the woman would be engaged in a conflict with the seed of the serpent. From the Garden of Eden to the cross of Calvary, the battle raged.

The birth of Jesus was foreseen by Abraham in his son Isaac. Abraham was old in years, and so was his wife Sarah, but God promised him that he would have a son. In this promised son, all of the nations of the earth would be blessed. That is why Jesus said that Abraham saw His day (John 8:56). In order for this child to be born, God had to touch the bodies of Abraham and his wife. Both were old and past their childbearing years. Sarah laughed when she was told that she would have a son, but Abraham believed God, and God touched his body and the body of his wife. She bore a son whom they named Isaac. The name Isaac means "laughter." God kept His promise and brought laughter to the home of Abraham. Every time Abraham saw his son, he saw a vision of Jesus.

The birth of Jesus was then foreseen by the prophet Isaiah. More than seven hundred years before Jesus was born, Isaiah said that God would give the Hebrews a sign. That sign was that a virgin would conceive and bear a Son (7:14). How strange this must have sounded to the people of that day! However, this was not just the word of Isaiah, but the holy, revealed Word of God Himself. Furthermore, Isaiah said that this Son would be Israel's King, that He would be identified with the Father and would even be Almighty God Himself (9:6).

Then the prophet Micah prophesied that Jesus would be born in the town of Bethlehem (Mic. 5:2), and the timing of His birth was predicted by the prophet Daniel. This birth was planned by God. It was foreseen by holy men of old and should not have been a surprise to Israel.

When the time for Jesus' birth came, it was seen by Joseph, who was to be the earthly father for our Lord. An angel appeared to him and revealed this part of God's plan so that it would not be a stumbling block that his espoused wife was to give birth. She was that virgin prophesied by Isaiah (Matt. 1:20–23).

The birth of Jesus was vital to the fulfillment of God's plan. God had to take upon Himself the robe of flesh and come down to man so that He could redeem this lost world.

The authenticity of the Old Testament has been verified throughout the ages. More than a dozen times, the New Testament tells of things that happened in the life of Jesus so the Scriptures "might be fulfilled" (Matt. 1:22; John 19:24), showing His fulfillment of an Old Testament prophecy. God keeps His Word, allowing it neither to fail nor to return to Him void (Isa. 55:11). The Old Testament would not be the true Word of God if Jesus Christ had not been born.

This world needed a Saviour, and it still does. In order to save sinners, Jesus had to come into the world, because only He could fulfill this need.

Mankind is destroying itself. The best efforts of the greatest minds have been futile in halting the corruption in the human race. There could be no hope without the intervention of God. When the hopes of Israel were gone, Jesus came to die for the salvation of men. As men turn further and further from God today, hope for the world is nearly gone. But Jesus is coming again, and this is our blessed hope (Titus 2:13)!

One of the most important doctrines in the Bible is the doctrine of the virgin birth. In order for Jesus to be the pure and holy Son of God, He had to be born of a virgin, a girl who had never known a man in a sexual way. The modernists have tried to deny and destroy this great truth by saying that it is impossible for a child to be born without a mother and a father, but *nothing* is impossible with God. God made the first man, Adam, out of the dust of the ground; he had neither a father nor a mother. If God can do that, then He can take a virgin womb and make a body for His Son without the aid of an earthly father. If God can reach down to lifeless clay and breathe into it the breath of life and cause that clay to become a living soul, then God can breathe on a virgin womb and bring forth the living, pure, holy Son of God.

Mary, the virgin, had found favor with God, and she was chosen by God for this special purpose. What an honor! We should be thankful for Mary, but we must not worship her. She is not the mother of God, but just an instrument that God used to bring His Son physically into this world.

God planted in her body the Seed of eternity and deity. Since this seed did not come from a sinful man, the sin nature passed down from Adam was not a part of Jesus' being, even during His time in the flesh on earth.

The angel plainly told Mary that the One conceived in her was of the Holy Ghost (Luke 1:35). Jesus is the virgin-born Son of God. There never has been, nor will there ever be, another birth like His.

One of the greatest victories that this world has ever known was the birth of Jesus. The Devil did everything in his power to stop it. He tried to corrupt the seed line, but God rolled up His sleeves and bared His holy arm. This victory was wrought by God and God alone. The Seed of the woman was finally here to start His mission of bruising the head of the serpent.

Long lay the world in sin and unbelief, needing a Saviour. The birth of Jesus not only prepared for the bruising of the serpent, but it also spelled the ultimate doom of sin. His death can save us from sin's penalty in Hell; His life and intercession can save us from the power of sin in our daily lives; and His return will rescue

His own from the very presence of sin, as He takes us to the Home He has prepared for us in Glory!

From the land of the living, God sent His holy angels to announce the arrival of His Son. They sang the glory down, "Praising God, and saying, Glory to God in the highest, and on earth peace" (Luke 2:13,14). Man's governments and even the religious systems are the cause of strife in this world, and both rejected the Prince of Peace. But He overcame them both to lay the foundation for lasting peace, and when He comes again, peace will reign for one thousand years!

When the shepherds heard what the angels had to say and returned to their flocks, they too were worshiping and praising God, for victory was won—a Saviour had been born. The long-awaited King and Saviour of the world had been born that night.

2

Subject: The Childhood of Jesus Christ

Text: Luke 2

   I. He Was Dedicated to God by His Parents (vss. 22–24).

  II. He Was Blessed by the Old Saints (vss. 25–39).

 III. He Had Good Characteristics as a Youth (vs. 40).

 IV. He Was Trained in the Ways of God (vss. 41, 42).

  V. He Had a Desire to Be in the Temple (vs. 46).

 VI. He Was Amazing to Others (vss. 46, 47).

VII. He Was Committed to Doing the Father's Business (vs. 49).

VIII. He Was Obedient to His Earthly Parents (vs. 51).

 IX. He Continued to Grow in the Things of God (vs. 52).

The Childhood of Jesus Christ

The Bible contains little about the childhood of Jesus.

He, like Isaac, had a silent boyhood. From the time He was born until He was baptized in Jordan, not much is said about His life; only the Book of Luke gives an account of it. Luke contains fifty-two verses that tell of His childhood. These verses cover His birth, His eighth day when He was circumcised and His fortieth day when He was brought into the temple to be presented to the Lord. From this time until He was baptized by John, Luke records only the incident in the temple when the twelve-year-old Jesus conversed with the so-called wise men of His day. Although we do not know much about what took place in this time period of His life, there are, nevertheless, some spiritual truths from His childhood that we can apply to our Christian lives.

No one should ever doubt the godly character of Mary and Joseph. They were among the godliest people of the Bible. They knew that He was the Son of the living God, and they counted it an honor and privilege to be used of God for the holy purpose of rearing God's Son. Joseph and Mary are great role models for parents in the world in which we live.

One of the first things that Mary and Joseph did was

to present Him to the Lord, meaning that they were putting their Son on the altar. They were giving Him back to the God who sent Him to them, in order that He might be used in God's service. Mary and Joseph were not selfish; they wanted God's will to be done in their lives and in the life of Jesus. In fact, they sacrificed their own plans and desires for the sake of what was best for this Son. May God grant parents today the same grace to give their children the best that God has for them. Although Mary and Joseph were not rich in the world's eyes, they were blessed and honored by God. Their sacrifice of two turtledoves was the offering made by a poor family, according to the Book of Leviticus; but they gave what they had, and when Jesus became a Man, He gave what He had—Himself.

Jesus as a Baby was blessed by the old saints of God. Simeon was a godly man, pure, just and filled with the Holy Ghost. He took baby Jesus in his arms and gave praise to the God of Heaven. An aged woman by the name of Anna, who was also pure and holy, gave praise and glory unto the Lord for Jesus. Our children need to be around such godly men and women and have their blessing and influence. I believe there was a soft place in the heart of Jesus for people who loved and served His Father.

Jesus was blessed with good character as a Child. He was strong in spirit, not being led astray by the things of this world. His inner man was strengthened by His Father. Young people today would do well to ask God to strengthen their inner man so that they will not be so easily led away from Him.

Wisdom is a great treasure from God. Knowledge can be gotten from man, but true wisdom can come only from God. Jesus was full of wisdom. Young people today could make the right decisions in life if they were filled with wisdom. In the Book of James, God promises to give us wisdom if we ask for it in faith (1:5–7).

One of the great things that marked the life of Jesus was the love and kindness that He showed to others. The grace of God was upon Him. The words that He spoke and the deeds that He did were all kissed with the dew of His grace.

Jesus was trained in the ways of God. He went with His parents to the Feast of the Passover every year. The Bible says that He went with His parents (Luke 2:41, 42), showing us that they taught Jesus not only by word, but also by example. Jesus saw them going, and their example made an impact on His life. The Bible says that they went every year; it was no hit-or-miss thing with them. Mary and Joseph knew that their responsibility was great before God. The only things about God and the Bible that children will know are what they see in their parents.

When it was discovered that Jesus was missing from the group of travelers that His family was with, He was found in the temple. He had a desire to be in the temple. When children see that church is important to their parents, it creates a desire in their own hearts to be faithful to the house of God. The first time Jesus was alone, the first place He went was the temple.

Jesus was amazing to others. They were astonished at His understanding and knew that He was special. He was blessed by God, and others knew it. We need young people who will storm this world and amaze people for the glory of God. The unsaved need to see that young people can live for God.

Faithfulness was also a great trait in the life of

Jesus. He was committed to God and was always about His Father's business. Many times Jesus made it plain that He did not come to do His own will or preach His own Word, but to do and be everything that His Father wanted Him to be. God will bless a person who is faithful. We need more faithful people in our churches today. Young people are committed to everything today but the Lord Jesus Christ. Faithfulness honors God, and God will honor faithfulness.

One of the Ten Commandments says that children are to honor and obey their parents. Jesus was an example in this. The Bible says that He was subject to His parents. Even though He was the Son of God, the Saviour of the world and the King of Kings, He was still subject to His earthly guardians.

Jesus had favor not only with God His Father, but also with His fellowman. It is very important that we fellowship with God and walk in His ways, but we must also remember that we are in the ministry of blessing and helping people. We need to be right not only with God, but also with people. We should love not only God, but also people. We need to fellowship not only with God, but also with people.

This is all that is said in the Bible about the life of Christ as a Child, but in this portion of His life, we find great spiritual truths that will make us better people if we will apply them to our lives! Jesus was characterized by these qualities throughout His life and was well prepared for what His Father wanted Him to do and be. Jesus is a good example not only in His preaching and holy living, but also in His childhood.

3

Subject: The Baptism of Jesus Christ

Text: Matthew 3:13–17

I. The Place of His Baptism
   A. The Meaning of the River Jordan
   B. The Mention of the River Jordan

II. The Preacher of His Baptism (John the Baptist)
   A. Filled With the Holy Ghost
   B. Cried Out Against Sin
   C. Preached Repentance

III. The Purpose of His Baptism
   A. To Show Substitutionary Death
   B. To Be Our Example

IV. The Picture of His Baptism
   A. Of His Death
   B. Of His Burial
   C. Of His Resurrection

V. The Power of His Baptism
   A. The Heavens Were Opened
   B. The Spirit of God Descended
   C. The Voice of God Was Heard From Heaven

VI. The Preparation of His Baptism
   A. For His Temptation
   B. For His Public Ministry

The Baptism of Jesus Christ

One of the most blessed events in the life of our Lord was His baptism in the Jordan River. This was a baptism not only of water, but also of the power of the Holy Spirit. After this, Jesus went forth to the wilderness for his forty-day battle with Satan and then into three years of public ministry. Before any person in the Bible did something great for God, he had a special time when God touched him and gave him His power for service. As we study the baptism of our Lord, we will see some things that can be applied to our lives today. How we need His touch!

The place where Jesus was baptized was the Jordan River. The name *Jordan* means "descender," because it starts north of the Sea of Galilee and descends to the lowest depression on the earth in the Dead Sea. It was and is the boundary line for the land of Palestine. Israel had to cross this river before they could enter the Promised Land.

The river Jordan is one of the most talked-about rivers in the Bible. It was the site of one of the most important scenes in the ministry of Elijah and Elisha. It was at the banks of this river that the chariot of fire parted Elijah from Elisha and the whirlwind swept Elijah up into Heaven, letting his mantle fall back to Elisha.

A captain of the army of Syria by the name of Naaman had leprosy. The man of God told him to go dip himself seven times in the Jordan River.

The river of Jordan speaks of self-denial, dying to self and living for God and His will. How there needs to be a river of Jordan in the lives of all of us today! There needs to be a time in our lives when we die to self and make up our minds that we are going to do God's will and find His perfect land of blessing for us. This was the place where Jesus was baptized, thereby showing the world that He had come not to do His own will, but the will of His Father who had sent Him (John 4:34). We could experience more of the power of the Holy Spirit in our lives if we would cross the river, die to self and do God's will.

The preacher at this baptism was John the Baptist. He was one of the godliest and fieriest men of the Bible. John was filled with the Holy Ghost from His mother's womb. His father and mother, who were servants of the Lord, had been told by an angel that this special child would be born unto them. It was foretold by the prophets that God would send His messenger to prepare the way for the Messiah; John was that voice that came out of the wilderness preaching repentance and righteousness.

John the Baptist's message was one of condemnation of the sins that had taken hold among even the religious leaders in Israel. He even called them a generation of vipers and warned them that God's wrath was coming to send judgment upon them.

He pressed upon them the urgency of their need to repent and told them to bring forth fruit that was evidence that they had.

Of course, along with judgment, he preached of God's provision for salvation. It was John who said by the banks of the Jordan, "Behold the Lamb of God" (John 1:29). John was sent to prepare the way of the Lord and make His paths straight. John was a Holy-Ghost-filled, sin-condemning, repentance-believing, Christ-honoring preacher of whom Jesus said that no man born of woman had ever been greater (Matt. 11:11). We need more preachers like John today.

One might ask why Jesus was being baptized. It would seem that Jesus, being holy, pure and sinless, would not need to be baptized. Baptism is something sinful men need to do, but Jesus knew what He was doing. Jesus was baptized by John for two reasons.

The first reason was to show that He was taking our place as sinners. He was born among sinners, lived among sinners, ate with sinners and even died among sinners. Thank God, He took our place as sinners! He became sin for us that we might be made righteous in His sight (II Cor. 5:21). Jesus is the great Substitute in whom we trust.

The second reason for His baptism was to show us an example. Jesus never commanded us to do anything that He would not do Himself. We are commanded to be baptized, and Jesus was not only our Substitute but also our Example.

In His baptism, He pictured what He had come to do: die, be buried and rise again. This is the very message of the Gospel.

Jordan is a picture of death. People often refer to their death by saying that they will cross the Jordan River. When Jesus was taken under the water, He was showing forth His death.

17

The time that He was under the water pictures His three days and three nights in the heart of the earth. He said the story of Jonah was a foreshadowing of this.

When John lifted Jesus out of the water, He was telling of His resurrection. A person's baptism is a testimony to the world that he is rising up to walk in the "newness of life" (Rom. 6:4), never to die again.

When Jesus came out of the water, the Bible says that the heavens were opened. God was about to show personally His pleasure with the obedience of His Son. He would do so in two ways.

First, the Holy Spirit came down in the form of a dove and rested on Him. This showed the power of the Holy Ghost coming down upon Him.

The dove in the Bible is a symbol of peace and purity. Noah released a dove from the window of the ark, and it came back with an olive branch in its mouth. It was a sign of peace—the Flood was over. It was also a sign of purity—the earth had been cleansed of its evil.

Like that dove in Noah's day, the Dove that came upon Jesus was a sign of peace and purity. Long lay this world in strife, and the only real peace it could ever know would come through this man Jesus. The dove would not light upon anything unclean. Jesus was the holy, pure, sinless, righteous Lamb of God. That is why Jesus could say when He went into the synagogue, "The Spirit of the Lord is upon me, because he hath anointed me to preach the gospel" (Luke 4:18). He had the Spirit's power upon His life.

Second, the Father expressed His pleasure audibly. One of the few times in the New Testament that God spoke from Heaven was at the baptism of Jesus. Here we see the Trinity in action: God the Father speaking from Heaven, God the Spirit coming down like a dove, and God the Son standing in the water. God spoke with a voice that shook the foundation of the earth and said, "This is my beloved Son, in whom I am well pleased" (Matt. 3:17). It is pleasing to God when we obey His commands. It also pleases God to send His power upon our lives.

The baptism of Jesus was preparing Him for what was ahead. After this, He fought the Devil for forty days. Then He began His public ministry for three years.

Although Jesus is God, He went against Satan in the power of the Holy Spirit. This shows us that we too can overcome the Devil, because the same power is available to us who are indwelt with the Spirit. We need the power of the Holy Spirit and the divine approval of God upon our lives so that we can stand against the temptation of the Devil.

Jesus also received this power of the Holy Spirit before He began His public preaching ministry. If the Son of God felt the need of this power before beginning God's work in this ungodly world, certainly we can only serve God in our public ministries when His power is upon us. We need obedience in the public testimony of baptism as well as in our private walk with God to get this power. We need this baptism of power in and upon us today as we serve God in this world.

4

Subject: The Temptation of Jesus Christ

Text: Matthew 4:1–11

I. The Avenue of Temptation
   A. The Devil's Timing
   B. The Devil's Tactics

II. The Application of the Truth
   A. The Truth Disrobed Satan
   B. The Truth Deterred Satan
   C. The Truth Defeated Satan

III. The Angels of Triumph
   A. They Were Encamped
   B. They Were Encouraging
   C. They Were His Escape

The Temptation of Jesus Christ

What a great contrast there is between our last scene of Jesus at the river Jordan and this one in the wilderness of temptation. Alfred Edersheim stated it this way in his book entitled *The Life and Times of Jesus the Messiah:*

> From the Jordan to the wilderness with its wild beasts, from the devout acknowledgment of the Baptist, the consecration and filial prayer of Jesus, the descent of the Holy Spirit and the heard testimony of Heaven to the utter forsakenness, the felt want and weakness of Jesus and the assaults of the Devil—no contrast more startling could be conceived.

From our human side of limited understanding, it is hard to see why Jesus was tempted. One might ask, "Why did Jesus have to go through this?" Jesus was the God-Man—He was God, yet He was man. He was God in His deity, but He took upon Himself the form of a servant; therefore, He was also Man. As Man, He could be tempted, and it was necessary for Him to be, for later the Bible declares that He was in all points tempted even as we are; yet, as God, He could not sin (Heb. 4:15). If He could not have been tempted, He would not have been Man; yet, if He could have sinned, He would not and could not have been God. He was Man, and He was tempted; He was God, and He *could not* and *did not* sin. It was absolutely impossible for Jesus to sin; He was the spotless Lamb of God.

Once again, we see that Jesus was our Example in all things. He showed us that if we follow His example, we can be victorious over the temptations of the Devil. We must see that victory is possible only through Him and His power. Just as David in the Old Testament was victorious over the giant in his day, so our Lord of the New Testament was and is the Champion over Satan, the giant of sin today, not only in His death and resurrection, but also in His life here on earth. As He had victory over Satan, so can we be victorious through His example.

Several lessons from this temptation can be applied to our lives today. Notice how Satan came to Jesus. The Devil came to Jesus right after a time of great blessing. Jesus had been baptized in Jordan, and the Holy Spirit had come down in power upon Him. What a time of glory and blessing this was in the life of our Lord! Then Satan came to Him. The Devil will not sit back and see God blessing our lives and not try to discourage us.

Not only was it a time of blessing, but it was also a time of physical weakness. Jesus had fasted for forty days, and the Bible says that He was hungry. When we are weak and tired, Satan will then come to us and try to pull us away from God. It is good to know that even this was all in the providence of God. The Bible says that Jesus was led of the Spirit; He was still in the will of God.

The tactics of the Devil have not changed. From the time he came to Eve in the Garden of Eden, to the temptation of our Lord, to the day in which we live, Satan uses the same old tricks to lead us into sin and rebellion. We see that the lust of the flesh, the lust of the eyes and the pride of life are still the avenues of Satan's temptation. The body, soul and spirit are the battlegrounds on which we fight against Satan and his onslaughts. In the three times the Devil came to Jesus, we see how he comes to us today.

In the first temptation, the Devil attacked His flesh. Jesus was hungry; He had fasted for forty days, and the Devil tried to get Him to turn the stones into bread. The Devil knows how to play on our flesh. We must keep our bodies under subjection and walk in the Spirit so we will "not fulfil the lust of the flesh" (Gal. 5:16). Our flesh will lead us away from God if we let it. Jesus knew that there was something in life more important than the flesh and its gratification, for Jesus said to the Devil, "Man shall not live by bread alone, but by every word of God" (Luke 4:4).

In the second temptation, we see that Satan tried to use pride to bring down the Son of God. The Devil will take us up in pride first; then he will cast us down in defeat. Jesus knew that the Devil gives only false pride, never reality. The Devil misquoted the Word of God. He did this when He came to Eve. Look out when Satan starts to use the Bible, because he will never get it right. Jesus rebuked Satan, telling him that He should not tempt the Lord God.

In the third temptation, we see the lust of the eyes. Here the Devil lied again by promising to give Jesus the earth if He would bow to him. The earth was not the Devil's to give. Satan will lie; he will promise things that he can never give. He can never give joy and peace. He just tries to tell us that if we will go his way, he can make us happy. This is his lie; do not believe it. In this temptation, Satan's true character comes out. His whole purpose in tempting us is to get us to turn our backs on God and to worship him. This is what the Devil got Eve to do, and it is what he tried to get Joseph to do. Jesus knew that no one was to be worshiped but God. It is to God that we owe our allegiance. He alone is the object of our worship. Our service is to Him and for Him.

What Jesus used to combat the Devil is available to all believers today. He did not use His power, His holiness or His wisdom, but rather He used His Word, the Word of God, the Sword of the Spirit. We have the Word of God today to help us stand against the wiles of the Devil. When Paul listed the armor of God in the sixth chapter of the Book of Ephesians, the only offensive piece was the Sword of the Spirit, the Word of God. This is what Jesus used, and we can use it too—it works!

Three times Jesus quoted the Word of God. The Scripture was hidden away in His heart. That is why the psalmist said, "Thy word have I hid in mine heart, that I might not sin against thee" (Ps. 119:11). The Word of God disrobed Satan, showing him for who he was and what he was up to. God's Word deterred Satan, as his plan was thwarted. And God's Word defeated Satan, putting him on the run. The Bible says that "the devil leaveth him" (Matt. 4:11). The only way to get rid of the Devil is to plead the blood and claim the Word of God.

After this battle with Satan, Jesus was ministered to by the angels of God. According to the promise of Psalm 34:7, the angels were encamped round about Jesus during His battle with the Devil.

They encouraged Jesus just as one of them would do

later in the Garden of Gethsemane (Luke 22:43). God promises that His angels will be there to minister in time of need (Heb. 1:14).

God did not abandon Him, but helped Him and strengthened Him. God will always come and help His children who trust Him. Psalm 91:11 prophesies that He will "give His angels charge over thee, to keep thee in all thy ways." The angels were His escape, as I Corinthians 10:13 promises: "There hath no temptation taken you, but such as is common to man: but God is faithful, who will not suffer you to be tempted above that ye are able; but will with the temptation also make a way to escape, that ye may be able to bear it." Luke says that "Jesus returned in the power of the Spirit" (4:14). There is a way out of temptation if we use God's Word and trust in His strength.

5

Subject: The Disciples of Jesus Christ

Text: Mark 3:13–19

I. The Call of His Disciples
   A. It Was a Personal Call
   B. It Was a Powerful Call
   C. It Was a Purposeful Call
II. The Character of His Disciples
   A. Their Names (Mark 3:13–19)
   B. Their Natures
      1. Human
      2. Weak
      3. Prone to Doubt
      4. Real People
III. The Conditions of His Disciples
   A. Forsaking the Cares
   B. Feeling the Cross
   C. Following the Christ

The Disciples of Jesus Christ

When Jesus began His public ministry, He called some men to help Him; these men are called disciples. The word *disciple* means "a follower and learner of Jesus." This is what they did—they followed Jesus and learned of Him. What a privilege it must have been to walk and talk with Jesus as He preached His messages and performed His miracles! One of the blessed truths of the Bible is that God can, will and wants to use human instruments to do His work and to carry out His plan. God could have used anything He wanted to use, but He chose to use humans, you and me, for His work. In this chapter, we will take a brief look at each disciple and also at some things that can be applied to our lives as we strive to be His disciples today.

The first thing we need to look at is the calling of His disciples. They did not choose to follow Jesus as an occupation; they did not ask Him if they could go along; they did not just decide to be disciples—they were *called*. Jesus Himself issued a call to them, for them and concerning them. He placed a claim on their lives; they were His disciples. He had made them and blessed them, and He had the authority to be the Lord of their lives. The greatest thing that ever happened to these men was the day each one heard and heeded the call that Jesus, the Son of God, placed upon his life. Thank God for the day He placed His calling upon our lives!

The call of Jesus to be His disciple is a personal one. He loves the masses, and He speaks and calls out to the masses; but when He wants to do a work in someone's heart and life, He calls and works on a personal basis. Jesus is a personal Saviour who loves and saves individuals. Jesus blesses us, uses us and works in us on a personal level. Jesus called them one by one.

When these men heard the call of the Master, they left what they were doing and followed Him. The call of Jesus is powerful. There was something in His voice and a look in His eye that they could not refuse.

When Jesus called His disciples, He had a plan for them, a purpose in calling them. Whatever their plans for life had been, those plans were not worth missing the plan that Jesus had for them. Jesus told them that if they would follow Him, He would make them fishers of men. Jesus put them in the people business. They would no longer live for themselves, but would live to glorify Jesus and to reach out to others. He knew they would live and minister in the midst of a lost and needy world. Jesus would go to Calvary to die for them, and He chose them to go tell this Good News. Our purpose today as disciples is to magnify Jesus and lift Him up to a lost and dying world, to throw out the lifeline of the Gospel and catch men for the glory of God.

Now let us see who these men were.

Simon Peter—the name *Peter* means "a rock." He was a fisherman by trade, but he left fishing to follow Jesus. It is amazing how Jesus took this man who was emotionally unstable and quick to go astray and called him "a rock," but that is what Jesus did. The cursing, unstable fisherman became the preacher of Pentecost and a pillar of the New Testament church, as well as a penman of the New Testament.

John—this man was called "the disciple whom Jesus loved." What a title! He is also called "John the Beloved." He was by no means perfect, but his heart and motives were pure. The love of God truly was "shed abroad in [his heart] by the Holy Ghost" (Rom. 5:5). Through the inspiration of the Spirit, he gave to us the Gospel of John, the three Epistles of John and the Book of the Revelation of Jesus Christ.

James—he is the brother of John and one of the sons of Zebedee. We know more of his parents and brother than we do of him. His personal deeds are not recorded, and he did not write a book, but we have no indication that he was discontented or unhappy. He was satisfied just to be a disciple. We do know that he was the first of the twelve disciples to die for the cause of Christ, being killed by Herod Agrippa (Acts 12:2).

Andrew—his name means "manliness," and what a man he was! He was the brother of Simon Peter. Some call him the first personal soul winner of the New Testament. When he met Jesus, the first thing he did was to find his own brother and bring him to the Saviour. He did not reach the pinnacle that Peter did, but Andrew had a part in everything that Peter accomplished. We never know what God will and can do with the people we reach for Him. Let us go fishing for men.

Philip—this man was from Bethsaida in Galilee and is often called "the disciple whom Jesus found." I call him "the reluctant one." According to Clement of Alexandria, tradition tells us it was he who asked if he could bury his dead before he followed Jesus. He was

33

slow to understand the truth, and he asked Jesus many questions; but Jesus used him, and he loved Jesus so much that he was willing to serve Him to the end. He died as a martyr at Hierapolis. One notable deed he did was to win another disciple named Nathaniel. These two men became partners in the Lord's work. It is a good thing to bring others to Christ.

Nathaniel—this name means "the gift of God." Truly every disciple is a gift of God. We are His disciples because we have received God's Gift, Jesus. Nathaniel is called the honest disciple; Jesus said that in this man there "is no guile!" (John 1:47). He is also known as Bartholomew in the first three Gospels. We could use more honest men today in the service of the Lord.

Thomas—he was also known by the name Didymus. The name *Didymus* means "double-minded." He no doubt was called this because of his tendency to be slow to believe. He has been called "doubting Thomas" many times, but we must remember that when he did see the living Christ, he confessed Him and said, "My Lord and my God" (John 20:28).

Matthew—his other name was Levi, which means "joined." Before he met the Lord, he was joined to the sinning ways of the world. He was a tax collector, a publican; this word was often associated with the word *sinner*. That is what we all are before we meet Jesus—sinners. However, his name was changed to Matthew, which means "the gift of Jehovah." He has blessed the Christian world not only by being one of the apostles of the early church, but also by giving us the first book of the New Testament, the Gospel of Matthew.

James the Less—he has been called "the less" because we know more of James the brother of John, not because he was unimportant to the Lord. He is also called the son of Alphaeus. We know nothing about him other than his name, except that he served the Lord and was faithful. We need more people today who are willing to serve Jesus unnoticed. We may be unnoticed on this earth, but in Heaven we will be rewarded and proclaimed. Whatever we do, we need to do it for the glory of God. Just bloom where you are planted and leave the rest to Jesus.

Judas Thaddaeus—*Judas* means "to praise the Lord," while *Thaddaeus* means "one who praises" or "tame of heart." Not much is known about his life and deeds; however, we can see in his name the purpose in life for all the followers of Jesus: to praise God from and with all of our hearts.

Simon the Canaanite—he was not called this because he was one of the sinful Canaanites that we read about in the Old Testament. Since the Hebrew word *qana* means "zealous," he is often called "Simon the Zealot." He was also called this because he was a member of a party of people that went by the name "zealot." The zealots were a sect of Jews that were opposed to the Roman domination of Palestine. When he became a disciple of Jesus, he used his zeal in the right way, serving the Lord with the same zeal with which he served the zealots. We should serve the Lord and give Him our all, more than when we served Satan. Most of us gave the Devil our best; let us do the same and *more* for Jesus.

Judas Iscariot—he is called "the traitor." He was the son of perdition, which means "eternal damnation." He was the one who betrayed Jesus for thirty pieces of silver. Judas went with and worked with the other disciples. He was so close to and yet so far from the Saviour and salvation. He is in Hell today because he had *religion in his head,* but he did not have *Jesus in his heart.* We need true disciples today.

We see that the disciples Jesus used to establish the church were just human beings chosen from normal walks of life for special service. They had the same weaknesses we experience, and they were prone to the same doubts we have. In short, they were real people who had an extraordinary Saviour.

We must meet a few conditions if we are going to be true disciples of our Lord. Jesus said that if we are going to be His disciples, we must deny ourselves. There is no room for selfish people in the work of God. We must get self out of the way before we will ever know the touch and power of God in our lives. If we are burdened with the cares of this life, we will not be effective.

We need not only to deny ourselves, but also to bear our cross. We are commanded to take up the cross (Matt. 16:24), to feel its weight in our lives. The word "cross" refers to more than our burden or affliction; it also speaks of our responsibility to live and to preach the good news of the Gospel. God has given us each a cross to carry. May we not lay it down until we receive our crowns.

The most important thing in our Christian lives is that we follow Jesus—not man, not the world, not the brethren, but Jesus, every day and every step of the way. Our Lord knows the way. He *is* the Way, and we will always travel the right road when we follow Him.

> I have decided to follow Jesus—
> No turning back; no turning back!

6

Subject: The Teachings of Jesus Christ—Part I
The Sermon on the Mount

Text: Matthew 5–7

I. The Happy Christian (5:3–12)
   A. The Foundation (vss. 3–6)
   B. The Fruit (vss. 7–12)

II. The Helping Christian (5:13–16)
   A. Salt for Fighting Decay (vs. 13)
   B. Light for Fighting Darkness (vss. 14–16)

III. The Holy Christian (5:17–48)
   A. In the Way We Think (vss. 22–28)
   B. In the Way We Talk (vss. 33–37)
   C. In the Way We Treat Others (vss. 38–48)

IV. The Humble Christian (6:1–34)
   A. In Our Deeds (vss. 1–4)
   B. In Our Devotions (vss. 5–18)
   C. In Our Desires (vss. 19–34)

V. The Honest Christian (7:1–29)
   A. The Fellowman (vss. 1–6)
   B. The Father (vss. 7–11)
   C. The Faith (vss. 13–27)

The Teachings of Jesus Christ
Part I

One could not study the teachings of Jesus without taking a look at what is called "The Sermon on the Mount." It is one of the greatest examples of the wisdom and truth of our Lord. It is a masterpiece. The Sermon on the Mount is to the New Testament what the Book of Proverbs is to the Old Testament. It tells how to live a life pleasing not only to the Lord, but also to our fellowman.

This great sermon of Jesus is not the Gospel, and it does not have to do with the way of salvation; however, it teaches righteous living in the kingdom of God. It describes the character of the truly righteous man as a result of his walking with God. It is a good guideline for daily godly living.

Matthew, in his Gospel, deals with the King and His kingdom. In chapters 5, 6 and 7, he deals with how people will and should live inside of the kingdom. We know that this kingdom has not come yet, but there are some wonderful truths in this sermon that can be applied to the Christian life today. It is not Christian law, but a practical lesson in righteous living.

Jesus begins by using the word "blessed." This word

means "happy." He tells His disciples that the way to be happy and blessed is to live righteously. People today are looking for happiness in all the wrong places. If we will live for God, we will find happiness. These verses of blessedness are called "the Beatitudes." They are not things to *do*, but things to *be*, things that we already are as disciples. They do not tell *how* to be happy, but *why* we are happy in the Lord.

Our attitude toward ourselves and our sinfulness is what is meant by the words "poor in spirit." We see our need for God's help and power in our lives. We know that we are not sufficient on our own, and our spirits cry out, "Lord, help us!"

Realizing our sinfulness and being sorry about it is what it means to mourn. We should not be proud of our sins.

To be meek is to be teachable. We are to submit ourselves to God and let Him work in our lives. A person who knows that he is nothing without God and is therefore submitted to Him will be a person who is happy. A happy person is one who is hungry and thirsty for the things of God in his life. Not only does our attitude toward ourselves need to be right, but our attitude toward God needs to be right as well. We will never be filled *with* Him until we are thirsty *for* Him.

In the first four beatitudes, we see the foundation of happiness. In the last four, we see the fruit or the results of being happy.

Thank God for those who know how to show mercy. No one will ever be happy until he learns how to love others and forgive those who do wrong to him. We need to be merciful.

Some people today think one can have happiness without holiness, but Jesus says in this Sermon that the pure in heart, the one who keeps his life clean, is the happy one. Holiness is happiness to him; because he is holy, he is happy.

The peacemaker is one who tries to bring others to Christ. Paul said that we are in Christ's stead beseeching men to be reconciled to God (II Cor. 5:20). Some of the happiest people I have ever met were soul winners. Outside of your own salvation, there is no greater joy than bringing others to Jesus.

The holy and happy one will not go untested. There will be those who will try to tear down and disturb your joy. If we live for the Lord and honor Him in our lives, we will be persecuted. The servant is not greater than his Master. If we are not happy in the Lord, we are not exercising our birthright as a child of the King.

In this great Sermon, Jesus deals not only with the happy Christian, but also with the helping Christian. Every Christian has a responsibility and a duty to the Lord and to this lost world. Our first responsibility is to be salt and light. The salt fights against the decay of sin, and the light battles against the powers of darkness. Not only is our world decaying, but spiritual darkness is settling in like never before. It is our duty to be salt and to shine in this world.

Concerning the salt of the earth, Dr. J. Vernon McGee said this:

> The problem today is that most church members have not only lost their tang as salt, but as pepper they have lost their pep also. We have very few salt-and-pepper Christians in our day. Now, salt doesn't keep fermentation and that type of thing from taking place, but it will arrest it. You and I ought to be the salt in the earth and have an

41

influence for good in the world.

This is our duty in the world today. Let us not lose our effectiveness or our testimony for the Lord. The only Bible some people will ever read is our lives. We should not only talk it, but also walk it. The deeds that come out of our lives ought to back up the words that come out of our lips.

Light works best in darkness. The darker the night, the brighter the light shines. We need to shine our light for the glory of God. Brighten the corner where you are—whether on the job, in the home or out in the community; wherever you go, just shine. When our oil is fresh and our globes are clean, our light will shine the brightest.

In the Sermon on the Mount, Jesus tells us how we can exercise holiness in our lives. He reminds us that we cannot be holy in action without being holy in thought. Some say that we are what we eat, and that may be true physically; but it is even truer spiritually that we are what we think. If we think on murder, then we are guilty of murder. If we look on women and lust after them in our hearts, we are guilty of adultery. All sin begins in the mind and then goes to the heart.

If sin is in our hearts, it will proceed out of our mouths. We, as children of God, should not swear or use oaths. We must watch our communication and ensure that it is honoring to the Lord.

If we have real holiness in our lives, it will affect the way that we deal with our fellowman. Some people claim a holiness and righteousness that does not show in the way they treat others. Jesus said we must love and forgive our enemies. We should do unto others as we would have others do unto us.

It is impossible to be right with God and not be humble. Humility is having the right attitude toward God and man without being proud of it. We can be humble in our deeds. God knows our service; we do not need to tell everyone about ourselves. When we give to others, we should not put on a show or turn on a bright light.

Then our devotions are to be humble as well. When we pray, we should not do so to be seen of men. When we fast, we should not do it so others will think that we really love God. Our Father who sees us in secret will reward us openly (Matt. 6:6).

A holy person is one who has his priorities in line; his desires will be humble. Serving the Lord and giving to His cause should be number one in our lives. We need to lay our treasures up in Heaven. We cannot serve two masters. If we will give our all to Jesus and be faithful to His work, He will take care of our needs. If He can see to it that the birds are fed and the flowers are watered, He can take care of His children.

The last thing that we see in this Sermon is the honest Christian. We should not judge others when there is sin in our own lives. Judging others will not remove the sin and problems that we have. We need to be honest and say, "It's not my brother or my sister, but it's me, O Lord, standing in the need of prayer."

We need to be honest not only with others, but also with God. We should tell God our needs and confess to Him our sins. Jesus said that the way to receive is to ask. The way to get the door opened is to knock. God is our Heavenly Father, and He knows how to give good gifts to His children.

Not only do we need to be honest with others and with God, but we also must be honest with ourselves about our faith. It is bad when Satan deceives us, and it is a sad thing when one has been deceived by sin, but the greatest deception is self-deception. Many are deceived when it comes to salvation. They have a form of godliness but do not have an inward reality. The only thing that is worse than going to Hell is going to Hell thinking that you were going to Heaven.

Jesus gives us a fourfold example of a true Christian in Matthew 7:13–27.

—He will travel the right road.

—He will produce the right fruit.

—He will claim the right truth.

—He will build on the right foundation.

If we will apply these truths to our lives, we will be more like our Lord and will know His full blessing in our lives.

7

Subject: The Teachings of Jesus Christ—Part II
Lord, Teach Us to Pray

Text: Luke 11:1–15

I. The Holy Approach (vs. 2—How Should We Begin Praying?)
   A. Acknowledge His Person ("Our Father")
   B. Acknowledge His Position ("in heaven")
   C. Acknowledge His Praise ("hallowed be thy name")
   D. Acknowledge His Purpose ("thy will be done")

II. The Humble Appeal (vss. 3, 4—For What Do We Pray?)
   A. Our Provision ("daily bread")
   B. Our Pardon ("our sins")
   C. Our Protection ("lead us...deliver us")

III. The Heavenly Answer (vss. 5–13—He Will Answer.)
   A. The Example (vss. 5–8, 11–13)
   B. The Encouragement (vss. 9, 10)

The Teachings of Jesus Christ
Part II

Prayer is one of the most important things in the life of a Christian. It is one of the most important subjects in the Bible, as well. One of the greatest things a Christian can be involved in is the activity of prayer.

Prayer was very important in the life of Jesus. He spent much time in prayer. He knew when to pray, how to pray and for what to pray. Jesus prayed in the desert, on top of the mountain and in the garden. He was a man of prayer.

The way Jesus prayed so impressed His disciples that they too wanted to pray. While Jesus was praying, they came to Him and asked, "Lord, teach us to pray" (Luke 11:1). Jesus taught not only with His lips, but also with His life. He taught not only with His words, but also with His walk. He taught not only with His exhortations, but also with His example. Jesus not only practiced what He preached, but He also preached what He practiced. What He lived, He taught; and what He taught, He lived. He not only taught us to love people, but He also loved people Himself. He not only taught us to be holy, but He also lived a holy life personally. He not only told us to pray, but He also prayed.

The greatest lessons on prayer one will ever hear are those taught by our blessed Lord. In this study, what has been called the "Lord's Prayer" is one of the examples of the teachings of Jesus on prayer; this is *not* the Lord's Prayer. The prayer that Jesus prayed in John 17 is the Lord's Prayer. This prayer was not prayed by our Lord, but rather it is the model prayer on which we are to pattern our prayers. He did not tell us to pray these exact words, but said "after this *manner* therefore pray ye" (Matt. 6:9). If we will pray as Jesus taught us in this prayer, we will experience the blessedness of having God answer our prayers.

The first thing that Jesus deals with in this prayer is how we should begin praying—how we should approach God. We must realize that we are on holy ground when we begin to pray. We are going before a holy God, the God of eternity. He is not "the old man upstairs," but God, the Creator of Heaven and earth, the King of Kings and the Lord of Lords.

God is our Father. Because of this personal relationship with Him, we can and should pray. As an earthly father loves his children, cares for his children and wants to bless his children, so does our Heavenly Father. He loves us. He cares about us. He knows our needs and wants to supply them. When we pray, we should be aware of this relationship. He is our *Father.*

Our Father is the Exalted One. He is high and lifted up. He is on the throne in Heaven and is not limited by time or by earthly surroundings. This is His position.

When we pray, we should start by praising God, not by asking Him for things. There is nothing wrong with asking; in fact, He tells us in this prayer that we can ask. But before we start asking, we should praise and adore Him. Oh, let us magnify the Lord.

The word "hallowed" means "let His name be holy." His name is set apart from all other names. It is different; it expresses everything He is in His character and attributes. In His name is lifted up who He is and what He is. He is love, and His name is love. He is holy, and His name is holy. Blessed, sanctified and holy be His name! Praise opens the door to prayer.

Before we can ever know the joy of answered prayer, we must submit to the will of God. God will never answer the prayer prayed from the rebellious heart. Most people will never know the will of God for their lives because they are not submitted to God and to what He wants them to do. Why should God give us more light when we are not using the light we already have? Let us not only recognize His position and praise His name, but also ask for His will to be done in our lives.

Some people teach that we as Christians today cannot use this prayer as our guide. They say that it is for the future kingdom only. One must realize, however, that the kingdom of God is a *present* reality as well as a *future* reality. Not only will Christ set up a future kingdom on the earth, but He has already established the present "kingdom of God...within you" (Luke 17:21).

Dr. Lehman Strauss, in his book entitled *Sense and Nonsense About Prayer,* says this concerning the kingdom of God:

> Actually, the kingdom of God is any sphere over which God rules. If we are resigned before God to give Him full allegiance and to do only His will, we can say the kingdom has come to us. The moment we pray, "Thy kingdom come. Thy will be done," we are at once submitting ourselves to implicit obedience to the will of

God. The kingdom of God is present in every believer in whose heart Christ reigns.

After we direct our prayer toward God, then we can humbly begin to pray for our needs. Our needs are many, but in this prayer Jesus puts them into three categories. The first is "our daily bread." This is a prayer for our provisions. We should look to God for even the food that goes into our mouths. God wants us to trust Him, not others or ourselves. We should depend upon Him for our every need. We must learn to live daily, pray daily, trust Him daily, die to self daily and walk with God daily. We should live one day at a time.

The second thing Jesus said we should pray for is our pardon. The old sin nature is present with us every day, causing us to sin and to fall short of God's glory. There is no one who does not need to confess his sins. David, in the Old Testament, said, "If I regard iniquity in my heart, the Lord will not hear me" (Ps. 66:18). We must keep the way clear. God will not answer the prayer prayed from a heart full of unconfessed sin. We all sin, and we must all confess our sins to God in prayer.

The last thing that Jesus said we must pray for is our protection. Not only should we pray and ask forgiveness for the sins that we have committed, but we must also pray and ask God to help us keep from sinning in the first place. We should begin every day of our lives on our knees, begging God to guide our paths in the right direction. The Bible says, "In all thy ways acknowledge him, and he shall direct thy paths" (Prov. 3:6). We need to pray every day that our Father will deliver us from the wiles and snares of the Evil One, the Devil.

In Luke 11:5–13, our Lord gives us two great examples of how God will answer our prayers. First, note the example of the friend. The one who was in bed got up to meet the need of his friend because his friend kept on asking and because he was his friend. Jesus is the dearest Friend we will ever have, and He will stick closer than a brother.

Second is the example of the good father. The father loves his son and will not give him something that will harm him. He will give his son that which is good for him. He will not give him that which will cause him evil, but that which will give him blessing and joy. Our God is in the bread, fish and egg business, not the stone, serpent and scorpion business. If we who are weak and carnal can love and care for our earthly children, how much more will our holy, sinless, unchanging Heavenly Father give us what we need? He gives good gifts. I find no fault in the way my Lord has taken care of me and supplied my every need.

The Lord adds His encouragement to get us to pray. Asking, seeking and knocking are the ways to have our prayers answered.

> God answers prayer in the morning;
> God answers prayer at noon;
> God answers prayer in the evening,
> So keep your heart in tune.

—Elsie Leslie

8

**Subject: The Teachings of Jesus Christ—Part III
Jesus' Teaching on the Holy Spirit**

Text: John 3; 14–16; 20

I. The Begetting of the Spirit (3)
   A. The Work of the Spirit (3:3–7)
   B. The Wind of the Spirit (3:8)
   C. The Witness of the Spirit (3:11; chs.14–16)
      1. A Sacrificial Death
      2. A Supernatural Love
      3. A Simple Salvation

II. The Blessing of the Spirit (14–16)
   A. The Blessing of His Person (14:16–18—Who He Is)
   B. The Blessing of His Presence (15:26, 27—Where He Is)
   C. The Blessing of His Purpose (16:7–15—What He Will Do)

III. The Breathing of the Spirit (20)
   A. The Breath of His Peace (vs. 19)
   B. The Breath of His Proof (vs. 20)
   C. The Breath of His Plan (vs. 21)
   D. The Breath of His Power (vs. 22)

53

The Teachings of Jesus Christ
Part III

We come now to one of the most blessed subjects of the Bible, the Holy Spirit. I do not know of anyone who can teach us any more about Him than Jesus, our Lord. The Holy Spirit is a major theme in the teachings of Jesus.

The Godhead, the Trinity, is manifested in three distinct Persons; God the Father and God the Holy Spirit are just as much God as God the Son is. All are holy, pure, just, loving, merciful and everlasting. This is one of the great mysteries of the Bible.

While He was on this earth, God the Son, Jesus, had a special relationship with the Holy Spirit. Jesus was conceived in the womb of the virgin by the Holy Spirit. When Jesus was baptized in the river Jordan, the Holy Spirit came upon Him like a dove. He was led by the Spirit and refreshed by the Holy Spirit on many occasions. The Holy Spirit anointed Jesus to preach the Gospel and to work miracles. He was raised up from the dead by the Holy Spirit. With this knowledge of the Holy Spirit, Jesus could lead His disciples into great depths of truth concerning Him.

The Gospel of John is a great book to use as a study

guide on the Holy Spirit. More is said about the Holy Spirit in the Book of John than in the other three Gospels. Approximately twenty times John's Gospel mentions the Holy Spirit. We will look at five chapters of this book and see who the Holy Spirit is and what His purpose is in our lives today.

In John 3, Jesus is teaching a man by the name of Nicodemus that it is through the Holy Spirit that a sinner is born into the family of God. Nicodemus was a leader of the Jews. He was a Pharisee and was very religious. He was a moral man who was respected, but Jesus had to tell him, "Ye must be born again." Nicodemus was not good enough in himself to go to Heaven or to enter into the kingdom of God. Even though he was a man of great learning, he did not understand this great truth. His mind, like those of all sinners, was darkened by Satan and by religious deception. But when he came to Jesus, who is the Light of the World, he found out that the only way a person can go to Heaven is to be born again of the Spirit. In a physical birth, seed is planted, conception occurs and life begins. Then, after much travail, there is a birth. So it is in a spiritual birth. The work of the Holy Spirit is to plant the seed of the Gospel into our hearts. He waters the seed, and through the travail of conviction there is a birth, and our spiritual life begins.

The Holy Spirit is likened to a wind in verse 8. The wind is unseen as it comes and goes, but it is very powerful. The Holy Spirit plays a major role in the salvation of sinners. He convicts men of their sins and enlightens their darkened minds. He reveals Jesus to a broken heart. When we are born into the family of God through Him, He baptizes us into the body of Christ. He dwells in our hearts by faith and seals us until the day of redemption. A person cannot be saved apart from the working of the Holy Spirit.

In verse 11, John speaks of the witness of the Spirit. This chapter contains some of the best known and most beloved verses of the Bible. He tells of Christ's sacrificial death by comparing it to Moses' lifting up of the brazen serpent in Numbers 21. This is testimony of the supernatural love of God for His creatures that offers them a simple plan of salvation—"whosoever believeth in him should not perish, but have everlasting life."

Chapters 14 through 16 of the Gospel of John are like three jewels in a gold setting. Here Jesus is preparing His disciples for the day when He will go back to be with His Father. He is telling these worried men that the Holy Spirit will abide with them and empower them to carry on the great work that He has given them to do. August Van Ryn, in his book entitled *Meditations in John,* says this concerning these three chapters in the Book of John:

> In chapters 14–16, our Lord has much to say of the ministry of the Holy Spirit. The believer is not called upon to go through life alone, but always has with him, by his side, One who is able to do for him all he needs. The Spirit ministers Christ to our hearts to keep us in communion with Him.

Thank God that the Holy Spirit has come and is with us today as we face the world and all of its temptations!

In chapter 14, John deals with the Person of the Holy Spirit—who He is. He is the Comforter. Jesus was getting ready to leave His disciples, and He wanted them to know that they would not be alone in the world. He promised them that He would not leave them comfortless. The word "comfortless" is the Greek word *orphanos,* from which we get our English word *orphan* or *fatherless.* Jesus said that He would not leave them without a Father, a Guide, a Friend. Jesus did not leave us like orphans—without Someone to comfort us.

The Holy Spirit is not only *the* Comforter, but He is also *another* Comforter. The word "another" here is the Greek word *allos,* which means "another of the same kind," or one just like Jesus. The Holy Spirit is as real as Jesus is. He is kind and loving just like our Jesus is. In fact, one of the reasons that the Holy Spirit came was to testify of Jesus (John 15:26).

The word "Comforter" is the Greek word *parakletos*, which means "called to one's side to aid in a time of trouble." John used this word again in I John 2:1 when he referred to Jesus Christ as being our Advocate. This is the same word, *parakletos.* Here it means "one that pleads another's cause." He is a Go-between, a Bridge Builder, our Heavenly Lawyer. We have a Comforter at the right hand of God up in Glory. We also have a Comforter in our hearts through the Person of the Holy Spirit.

In John 15, Jesus deals with the presence of the Holy Spirit. Jesus said, "I will send unto you from the Father" (vs. 26). He made His disciples a promise that they would not be alone or without a Comforter. The disciples would never be without a witness on this earth. They would never be without the Spirit of truth who would testify of Jesus to their hearts and produce His image in their lives. Once again we see the Trinity. Jesus is speaking of the Holy Spirit, and he says that the Spirit "proceedeth from the Father." In this verse we have Gsod the Father, God the Son and God the Holy Spirit.

Jesus always keeps His promises. If He says that He

will do something, then He will do it. On the day of Pentecost (fifty days after the resurrection), He sent the Holy Spirit to indwell His disciples and all of the saved in these days of grace.

> Oh, spread the tidings 'round
> Wherever man is found:
> The Comforter has come.

> —Frank Bottome

In John 16, Jesus deals with the purpose of the Holy Spirit. What will He do when He is come? The work of the Spirit is given in a threefold manner. First, Jesus said that He would reprove the world of sin and of righteousness and of judgment (vss. 8–11). The word "reprove" is the Greek word *elegcho,* which means "to rebuke, expose or cross-examine; to place under conviction." The Holy Spirit will show the sinner that he is lost and unrighteous and that he will face the judgment of God.

Second, the Holy Spirit will guide the saved into all truth (v. 13). He is the Spirit of truth and will not lead us into sin or ungodliness. The Spirit will not deceive us; rather, He will lead us in the paths of righteousness for the sake of our Heavenly Shepherd (Ps. 23:3). The word "guide" is the Greek word *hodegeo,* which means "to lead the way." God's children do not have to worry about getting lost, because His Holy Spirit is leading the way. "Walk in the Spirit, and ye shall not fulfil the lust of the flesh" (Gal. 5:16).

Third, the Holy Spirit will testify of Jesus. He will not speak out of Himself; what He says will be from Jesus. The Spirit will not brag on Himself; He will point men to Jesus. When He is in control of the saint, He will cause him to speak of Jesus and to point men to the bleeding Lamb of God.

In the Steps of the Master

We have seen in this study that the Holy Spirit is the begetting Spirit and the blessing Spirit; now let us see that He is also the breathing Spirit. In John 20, the disciples were in a secret place for fear of the Jews. The doors were shut, and the disciples were afraid. Then Jesus came and stood in their midst. When they saw Him, they were glad, and their sorrow was turned into joy. Jesus spoke peace to their souls, gave proof of His identity and gave them His plan for their lives. He sent them just as the Father had sent Him.

But the greatest thing He did for them that night was that He breathed on them and said, "Receive ye the Holy Ghost" (vs. 22). W. E. Vine, in his *Expository Dictionary of New Testament Words,* said this concerning the word *breathe:*

> "To breathe upon" is used of the symbolic act of the Lord Jesus in breathing upon His apostles the communication of the Holy Spirit.

There is no substitute for the breath of God upon our lives. How we need His power in our preaching, in our praying and in our daily lives! May the Holy Ghost breathe on us in these last days!

9

Subject: The Miracles of Jesus Christ—Part I Concerning Nature

Text: John 2, 6, 11, 21

I. He Turned Water Into Wine: He Is My Satisfaction (2:1–10).
   A. The Want (vs. 2)
   B. The Water (vs. 7)
   C. The Wonder (vss. 9, 10)

II. He Fed the Five Thousand: He Is My Sustenance (6:5–14).
   A. The Hungry Crowd (vs. 5)
   B. The Helping Child (vs. 9)
   C. The Holy Christ (vss. 6, 11, 12)

III. He Walked on the Water: He Is My Serenity (6:18–21).
   A. He Conquered the Sea (vs. 19)
   B. He Came to the Ship (vs. 19)
   C. He Calmed the Saints (vss. 20, 21)

IV. He Raised Up Lazarus: He Is My Saviour (11:1–43).
   A. His Pity (vss. 3, 5, 33, 35, 36)
   B. His Purpose (vss. 4, 11, 15, 23, 25, 26)

V. He Put Fish on the Fire: He Is My Supply (21:5–14).
   A. His Concern (vss. 4, 5)
   B. His Command (vss. 6–10)

C. His Call (vs.12—"Come and dine")

The Miracles of Jesus Christ
Part I

When John the Baptist was in prison, he sent someone to ask Jesus, "Art thou he that should come, or do we look for another?" (Matt. 11:3). Jesus sent John a message that "the blind receive their sight, and the lame walk, the lepers are cleansed, and the deaf hear, the dead are raised up, and the poor have the gospel preached to them" (vs. 5). No one could do these miracles except the Christ—Jesus, the Son of God. Jesus was a man approved of God by signs, wonders and miracles.

In the next three chapters, we will study the miracle ministry of Jesus. He was the miracle-working Son of God. The Greek language has two different words which are translated *miracle*. The first one is the word *dunamis* which means "power, inherent ability or supernatural work," or something that only God could do.

The second is the word *semeion,* which means "a sign, mark or token as a result of the supernatural power that has been displayed." This word is akin to the word *wonder.* Together these words form a wonderful picture of the miracles of Jesus. He had inherent ability and divine power. He did things that only God could do, things that serve as a mark, sign and token that He is the Son of God who came to meet the needs of a lost world.

In this chapter, we will look in the Gospel of John at the miracles of Jesus concerning the things of nature. In John 2, Jesus began His miracle ministry by turning the water into wine. This was not an intoxicating beverage, because that would go against Proverbs 23:31. It was the purest fruit of the vine, but we will use the word in our Bible.

In this miracle, the token or sign that Jesus left was that He can satisfy the soul—He is our joy. Wine in the Bible is a sign of two things: joy and the Holy Spirit. Jesus was invited to a marriage that was taking place at Cana. When the time came to celebrate this union of two happy young people, there was too little wine, and it was consumed before the celebration ended. Everyone seemed to be disappointed. Mary, the mother of Jesus, came to her Son and said, "They have no wine."

Is that not a picture of people's lives today—no joy or satisfaction? Note that there were six water pots. Six in the Bible is the number for sin or man. These water pots were made of stone. The stone is a picture of hard, cold, dead, empty people. Notice also what Jesus said: "Fill the waterpots with water." Water is a type of the Word of God and the Holy Spirit.

When the ruler of the feast had tasted the water that was made wine, he did not know what it was or from where it had come. Until a person's eyes have been opened by the light of the Gospel, he cannot know the joy that Christ's salvation brings. The servants knew the Master and what He had done. They knew what it was and from where it had come. The Master had touched the water and made it wine. The wine was so good that the governor of the feast said that most people give the best wine first, but "thou hast kept the good wine until now" (vs. 10).

Thank God for the day He came into our cold, dead, empty lives, took His Word and, through the power of the Holy Spirit, changed our water into wine and gave us His "joy unspeakable and full of glory" (I Pet. 1:8). The Devil gives his best first, and when it is all gone, he gives his worst. However, for those who know the Joy Maker, Jesus, the best is yet to come. He is our Satisfaction.

In John 6, we find the account of Jesus taking five loaves and two small fishes and feeding a hungry multitude of five thousand men plus women and children. This is a picture of our world today—hungry. This lost world is trying everything to find joy and fulfillment. There is a longing in their souls that can be filled only by the Bread of Life, Jesus, the Son of God.

Jesus received five loaves of bread and two small fish. He took this bread and fish and blessed them; then he broke them and gave them to the disciples so that they could feed the crowd.

This miracle contains a twofold picture. The first is that Jesus is that Bread that God blessed and broke on the cross of Calvary. It is enough to feed every hungry sinner who will come to the Master's table. The second is that God can take our bread, our life and our talents that He has given us and can bless them. Jesus can take our lives and use them to bless and meet the needs of this lost, hungry world. He is our Sustenance.

Verses 18–21 of chapter 6 tell of another miracle of our Lord. This time He walked on the water. He has power over one of the greatest forces of nature, the sea.

In the Steps of the Master

After He had fed the people, Jesus told His disciples to "get into the ship, and to go to the other side" (Mark 6:45). As a result, they got in a storm. Jesus had gone up into the mountain to pray, and while they were down there going through the storm, He was up there praying for them. When their darkest hour came and it looked as if they were going down, there came Jesus, walking on the waves. The very thing they thought would be their destruction was Jesus' means of getting to them as He walked upon it.

He is not only the Wine Maker and the Bread Giver, but He is also the Wave Walker. He can calm the storms that rage in our lives. He is our serenity; there is peace in Him.

One of the most blessed of all the miracles that Jesus performed was His raising of Lazarus from the dead, a miracle recorded in John 11. Jesus loved Lazarus and his two sisters, Mary and Martha. He would often stay with them when He was going through Bethany.

Jesus was grieved in His spirit when He heard that Lazarus was sick and dying, but in order that He might prove to them that He was the Son of God, He waited until Lazarus had been dead for four days before going to his grave. When He arrived at the tomb of the one He loved, He prayed one of the most earnest and precious prayers ever uttered by the lips of any man. Jesus called Lazarus by name, and Lazarus came forth bound in his graveclothes. Then Jesus said, "Loose him, and let him go" (vs. 44). Truly Jesus is "the resurrection, and the life" (vs. 25)!

We all were dead in trespasses and sins. Then He came to us and called us, and we believed on His name. Now we have been resurrected from death unto life. A person has never really lived until he has been raised by the miracle-working power of Jesus, who is "the way, the truth, and the life" (14:6). This miracle shows that He is our Saviour.

In chapter 21, we have the last miracle recorded in the Gospel of John. The disciples had been fishing all night, and they had caught nothing.

Standing on the seashore was their Friend and Master, Jesus. He was concerned and wanted to meet their need. He told them to cast their nets on the right side of the ship. We need to learn from this text that if we expect to be fruitful in the Lord's work, we must do it on the *right* side and in the *right* way. When they followed the Master's command, they caught a great draught of fish.

Jesus told them to bring their fish and "come and dine" (vs. 12). When they arrived on shore, He already had fish on the fire. Jesus is well able to meet our needs and supply them. He will meet the needs of His people, even if He has to perform a miracle. He is the miracle-working Son of God.

10

**Subject: The Miracles of Jesus Christ—Part II
Concerning the Human Body**

Text: Mark 1, 2, 5, 7, 10

I. He Calmed the Fever: I Can Be Healed (1:29–31).

II. He Cleansed the Leper: I Can Be Clean (1:40–45).

III. He Corrected the Cripple: Now I Can Walk (2:1–12).

IV. He Cast Out the Demons and Devil: I Can Be Free
(5:1–20).

V. He Cured the Issue of Blood: I Can Feel and Know I'm
Saved (5:25–34).

VI. He Cheated Death: I Can Live (5:35–43).

VII. He Converted the Deaf and Mute: I Can Hear and Talk
With God (7:32–37).

VIII. He Conquered Blindness: Now I Can See (10:46–52).

The Miracles of Jesus Christ
Part II

As we come to the second part of our study on the miracles of Christ, we will study eight miracles in the Gospel of Mark that Jesus performed concerning the human body. Jesus created the human body, and He can heal or fix what goes wrong with it. In every miracle is a lesson to be learned.

Not only is He the Healer of the body, but also of the soul. He gives not only a physical touch, but also a spiritual touch. When He performed a physical miracle, He also preached a spiritual truth. If all a person sees is the physical healing, he has missed the main spiritual teaching. In every miracle in which Jesus healed a person's body, there was a picture of what He can do and will do in the spiritual realm in the area of salvation.

Mark 1:29–31 show Jesus calming the fever of Peter's mother-in-law. A fever is a result of an infection, and an infection in the Bible is a type of sin. All of humanity has been infected by the disease of sin, and the fever of rebellion rages in all our souls. We are sinners by birth, by nature and by choice. The Bible says, "All have sinned, and come short of the glory of God" (Rom. 3:23). If someone asks what he has to do to be a sinner, the answer is simple—just be born of two human parents into this sin-cursed world. However, all one has to do to become a saint of God is to be born again by the power and grace of God. Jesus said, "Ye must be born again" (John 3:7).

Mark 1:30 says that "anon they tell him of her." This word "anon" means "immediately, at once or shortly." They did not delay in telling Jesus of her fever. What a blessed woman she was to have someone who would tell Jesus of her sickness. Thank God for people who will pray for those who stand in need of a touch from the Saviour. Jesus answered their prayer. He took her by the hand and lifted her up.

What a wonderful picture we have here of Jesus saving a sinner! He reaches down His hand and lifts us up out of the miry clay and out of the depths of sin. When Jesus touched her, immediately her fever left her, and she served them. I am glad that when Jesus saves a sinner, it happens right then and there! After Jesus saves us, we ought to be so thankful that we will serve Him and thank Him for what He has done.

In this miracle, we see the spiritual truth that there is healing for the soul. Jesus is the only one who can calm the raging fever of sin. The Bible says, "Who his own self bare our sins in his own body on the tree, that we, being dead to sins, should live unto righteousness: by whose stripes ye were healed" (I Pet. 2:24).

In Mark 1:40 Jesus cleanses a leper. In the Bible, leprosy is a type of sin and its results. Note the following things about leprosy and sin.

—Leprosy begins in a small way; so does sin.
—Leprosy will always spread; so will sin.
—Leprosy always causes separation; so does sin.
—Leprosy, if left alone, will be fatal; so will sin.

Every person born of Adam's race is separated from God and is contaminated by the disease of sin. If something is not done about it, man will die in his sin and will go into a Christless eternity. Thank God that there was hope for the leper, and there is hope for the sinner. That hope is Jesus Christ. He and He alone has the power to cleanse us from all our sins and to wash us in His blood.

When this poor soul was cleansed by Jesus, he could not help but tell it. Verse 45 says that he began "to blaze abroad the matter." Like a machine gun blazing bullets, like a fire ripping through a forest, he could not hold it back. Now he was clean! Now he could go home and fellowship with his family! When a person meets Christ and is washed from his sin, then he can sing,

> What a wonderful change in my life has been wrought
> Since Jesus came into my heart!
> —R. H. McDaniel

In Mark 2:5, we see Jesus healing the man who was sick of the palsy. In this text, we can see what sin does to every man. It disables him; it cripples him. He cannot work or walk. All that this man could do was lie on his bed. He could not help himself.

This is true spiritually of men today who are lost in their sins. They are crippled and cannot walk with a holy God because of sin. A person who is a sinner cannot help himself. He is like the Ethiopian eunuch in Acts 8:31, who said to Philip, "How can I, except some man should guide me?" This poor man could not get to Jesus by himself. He needed some man to help him. It is always a blessing when we see how God can use human instruments in reaching people and making the difference in their lives. The crippled man's friends could not heal him, but they knew Someone who could. I am glad that I know Someone who can say to a world crippled by sin, "Take up thy bed, and walk."

When the people saw what Jesus had done and the great change in this man's life, they were amazed and glorified God. It is always amazing to see how God can touch and save a person who is disabled by sin and unable to walk straight, and then to see him walking and praising God. Only Jesus can make the lame to walk. Only He can take a life crippled by sin, straighten it out and give the individual the power to walk with Him throughout the rest of his life.

In Mark 5:8, Jesus cast the Devil out of the wild man of the Gadarenes. This man was made wild and untamable by sin. He was full of the Devil.

The reason we see such ungodly and diabolical sins today is because people are full of Hell and the Devil. A person controlled by Satan will do anything, no matter how sinful and shameful. Today in America, people are running wild. Rock music, drinking and sexual perversion—all of this is taking its toll on our country and our families. *There is hope!*

The Devil is no match for the Saviour. Jesus has power and authority over Satan and his demons. Jesus came to destroy the works of the Devil (I John 3:8). He came to set the captive free. Only He can break the chains of sin. Only Jesus can speak peace to the troubled soul. Through His shed blood and spoken word, He can take the Devil out of lost souls and take up His abode in them through the Person of the Holy Ghost.

Notice the change in this man's life. Before Jesus came, he was wild and could not be tamed. He was crying and even doing harm to himself. After Jesus passed by and set him free, he was found sitting at the feet of Jesus, clothed and in his right mind. Oh, what a difference since Jesus passed by!

The message in this miracle is that because of Jesus and through Jesus the sinner can be set free by the truth and power of God. "If the Son therefore shall make you free, ye shall be free indeed" (John 8:36).

Mark 5:25–34 gives the account of the woman with the issue of blood. In her case, we can see the plight and condition of every sinner. Her sickness caused her suffering. People in this world today are suffering because of sin. Not only did she suffer from her sickness, but she also "suffered many things of many physicians" who could not heal her. In fact, the Bible says she "spent all that she had, and was nothing bettered, but rather grew worse" (vs. 26).

So many today are looking for something and trying everything in this old world to find relief from the suffering of sin. They are not getting better; they are getting worse, and, in the process, it is costing them everything. The world does not have the answer.

The turning point in this woman's life was when she heard of Jesus. Oh, happy day when the good news that Jesus is passing through reaches the sinner! When she heard, she came. When she came, she touched. When she touched, she felt. When she felt, she fell down at His feet. When she fell, she told Him all the truth. Jesus did not rebuke her; rather, with tender lips, He said, "Go in peace, and be whole of thy plague" (vs. 34).

Hallelujah, what a Saviour! A sinner today, by faith, can reach out and touch Jesus. There is only one way to touch Him—just believe when you call on His name.

When we come to Mark 5:35–43, we see the ultimate

price of sin: death. The Bible says, "The wages of sin is death" (Rom. 6:23). "The soul that sinneth, it shall die" (Ezek. 18:4). "So death passed upon all men, for that all have sinned" (Rom. 5:12). "Sin, when it is finished, bringeth forth death" (Jas. 1:15). Every person who is without Christ is "dead in trespasses and sins" (Eph. 2:1).

The Bible speaks of a threefold death: spiritual death, physical death and eternal death. All of this is a result of sin; but, thank God, Jesus is the resurrection and the life (John 11:25)! Here in this text, He robbed death of another victim. Jesus took the young girl by the hand and spoke words of life to her soul, and she arose and walked.

The father of this child was able to say about his daughter the same thing that the father of the Prodigal Son could say about his wandering boy: "For this my son was dead, and is alive again" (Luke 15:24). Jesus gives not only physical life, but also spiritual life. Jesus said, "The words that I speak unto you, they are spirit, and they are life" (John 6:63). As the songwriter Philip P. Bliss said, "Sing them over again to me, wonderful words of life."

A person has never lived until Jesus speaks the words of life to him and he walks in the newness of life. There is no life outside of Jesus Christ, for He is "the way, the truth, and the life" (14:6).

In Mark 7:32–37, we see two things that a sinner cannot do. He cannot hear God or talk to God until he has met Jesus Christ, who opens the person's ears and loosens his tongue. Before we met the Lord, we were deaf and mute to the things of God. But He is able; He can touch our ears and loosen our tongues, and we can have perfect fellowship with our Lord. Because of

Jesus, God can hear what I speak to Him, and I can hear what He speaks to me.

Mark 10:46–52 records the last miracle that Jesus performed concerning the human body in this Gospel account. Here Jesus opens the eyes of blind Bartimaeus. In the other miracles, we have seen what sin does to and in our lives. It is no different in this miracle.

This man was blind. Satan uses sin to blind us. Paul says that "the god of this world hath blinded the minds of them which believe not" (II Cor. 4:4). The sinner is blinded to his sins and to the goodness of God toward him.

This man began to cry to Jesus for mercy. Jesus stood still, called for him and gave him his sight. The greatest of all miracles is when Jesus, who is the Light of the World, touches our blinded eyes and we come to the light of His Word and He saves us by grace. As Charles H. Gabriel wrote in his great hymn, "From shades of night to plains of light, oh, praise His name, He lifted me." Thank God for the day when Jesus passed by.

11

Subject: The Miracles of Jesus Christ—Part III
Concerning Salvation

Text: Luke 15, 19, 22

I. The Lost—He Is the Finder of Sinners (15).

    A. He Was Rebellious (vs. 13).

    B. He Was Regretful (vs. 17).

    C. He Was Righteous (vss. 22–24).

II. The Little—He Is the Friend of Sinners (19).

    A. He Was Little (vs. 3).

    B. He Was Loaded (vs. 2).

    C. He Was Lost (vs. 7).

    D. He Was Longing (vs. 3).

    E. He Was Liberated (vs. 9).

III. The Loser—He Is the Forgiver of Sinners (23).

    A. He Was Defiled (vs. 33).

    B. He Was Dying (vss. 40,41).

    C. He Was Desperate (vs. 42).

    D. He Was Delivered (vs. 43).

The Miracles of Jesus Christ
Part III

In this part of our study, we will see the greatest miracle that Jesus performed while He was on the earth. In fact, He is still performing this miracle today, and that is the miracle of saving sinners. This is the reason Jesus came. He was more than a good teacher, more than a healer of sick bodies and more than a helper of the needy. He was and is the Great Saviour of the world.

He did not come to call the righteous to repentance, because they that are whole need not a physician. Instead, He came to call sinners unto repentance (Luke 5:31, 32). Jesus came "to seek and to save that which was lost" (19:10). Lost was this world, and lost were you and I. Jesus left Heaven and the ivory palace of Glory and came into a sin-cursed world, not to restore world order, not to build a religious kingdom and not to deliver the Jews out of Roman bondage. He came to seek and to save, to love and to lift, to find and to forgive the sinner. He is the Seeking Shepherd and the Searching Saviour.

While Jesus was on this earth, He was accused of being a friend of sinners (7:34). They said, 'This man eats with sinners; this man receiveth sinners; this man is a guest of sinners.' They were right. Thank God, He was and still is today!

In the Gospel of Luke, there are three wonderful examples of how Jesus saves the sinner. In these examples, we will see whom He saves, where He saves and how He saves. Truly salvation is the greatest of all miracles!

Luke 15 gives the parable of the lost son. In fact, this whole chapter is a picture of a lost sinner and the desire of Jesus to save him. There are two other illustrations before the Prodigal Son.

First we see the lost sheep. Isaiah 53:6 says, "All we like sheep have gone astray." This sheep was lost from the fold and the protection of the shepherd. Then the shepherd went looking for this sheep. He found the sheep, put it on his shoulders and brought it back safely home. Every person who knows not the Saviour is like this lost sheep. Jesus, the Great Shepherd, is looking and seeking to save.

Second is the lost coin. This coin was lost among the rubbish of the house. This is a picture of sinners who are lost in our homes and in our churches today. This woman pictures the church, the bride of Christ, through whom the Holy Spirit is sweeping and seeking the lost. Jesus said, "When he [the Spirit of truth] is come, he will reprove the world of sin" (John 16:8). Jesus sent the Holy Spirit on the day of Pentecost, and since that day He has been seeking out a bride for the Lord Jesus.

The third parable is about the lost son. In this parable, we have one of the greatest pictures of the lost sinner in the entire Bible. In the life of this son, we can see what sin is and what it does to people's lives.

Sin is rebellion, and it will lead men astray. Sin will cost men everything and will make a mockery and a misery out of one's life. This boy was lost; he was lost to home, family, peace and the father's care—and so is everyone outside of Christ. Then he came to himself. Oh, happy day, when sinners awaken and come to themselves and realize their need of the Saviour!

In the illustration of the lost sheep, we see a picture of God the Son; in the story of the lost coin, we see a picture of God the Spirit as He works through the church; and in the parable of the lost son, we see a picture of God the Father. What a picture of the Trinity we have in Luke 15! All of the Godhead have a part in salvation. God the Father thought it. God the Son bought it. God the Spirit wrought it. Salvation was planned, provided and performed by the Trinity.

Jesus is the Finder of sinners. He knows where to look. He knows whom and for what to look. Some were by the sea. Others were by the wayside. Some were on the mountains, and others in the lowest valleys. Some were on the tempestuous sea, while others were in the sands of guilt and despair. Wherever they were, He loved them, He found them and He saved them. Jesus is the Finder of sinners.

When the lost son came home, his father restored him to the family and gave him a robe, a picture of the righteousness imputed to those who receive Christ. There was great joy in the house. It is shouting time in Heaven (and it should be on the earth also) when sinners come home to God. Oh, "happy day, when Jesus washed my sins away," wrote Philip Doddridge.

One of the sweetest examples of Jesus' saving sinners is found in Luke 19. This is the story of how Jesus met Zacchaeus and how Zacchaeus met Jesus. Zacchaeus was short in stature, but although he was little in height, he was big in being lost. He may have been a short man, but he was a tall sinner. No matter how tall or short we are physically, all are sinners and have "come short of the glory of God" (Rom. 3:23).

Zacchaeus was a tax collector. He was rich in this world's goods; but no matter how rich one is in this world, if he has never met the Lord Jesus, he is bankrupt concerning the next world, and he is lost. A number of people are so concerned about how much they can get down here that they have nothing to their credit up There. One cannot buy his way into Heaven. Salvation can be bought and paid for only by the blood of the Lamb.

The Bible does not say what it was, but something stirred the heart of Zacchaeus to want to see Jesus. A person who is not under conviction will not be seeking God. However, when the Holy Spirit makes one thirsty, that person goes looking for the water. Maybe Zacchaeus had heard about Jesus from someone whom Jesus had touched. Maybe he had seen the difference in the life of someone who had met the Lord. Whatever it was, blessed be the day when he went to see Jesus.

Zacchaeus climbed up a tree so he could see Jesus, and Jesus came to that tree. Then when Jesus called him, Zacchaeus came down from the tree and gladly received the Saviour. A sinner can go only so far, and then Jesus must make his move toward the sinner. After the Lord makes His move, the sinner must receive and obey the command of Jesus Christ in order to be saved.

Notice the threefold result of salvation in the life of this little man when he was set free by Jesus. First, there was joy. Second, there was a desire to take Jesus home to his family. Third, there was restitution. There was a great change in the life of Zacchaeus. Before he met the Lord, he was a little man. After he met Jesus, he was a big saint. Before, he was rich in the things of the world; but afterward, he was rich in Jesus. Truly, Jesus is the Friend of sinners! He is the dearest Friend one will ever have, a Friend "that sticketh closer than a brother" (Prov. 18:24). Oh, how He loves sinners and longs to save them by His grace! The hymn writer Charles W. Fry wrote, "I have found a Friend in Jesus; He's everything to me. He's the fairest of ten thousand to my soul."

As we come to Luke 23, we are gathered around the cross on which our Saviour died. We notice that on each side of our Lord is a malefactor (a criminal). These men were found guilty in a court of law for going against the law of the land. They were among the losers of society. There was another one scheduled to die, a murderer by the name of Barabbas. But he was released, and Jesus was to die in his place on his cross.

One of the malefactors was bitter. He had no respect for or realization of who Jesus was. He railed on Him and in mockery questioned His deity and reality. He plainly rejected the crucified Christ.

The other malefactor was touched by watching Jesus die for the sins of the whole world. He saw that he was a sinner and was on the verge of dying. He rebuked the other criminal. He realized that this Man, the Christ, was sinless and pure and acknowledged that He was the King that would come into His kingdom.

This malefactor had a great, desperate desire to be saved and to be a part of this kingdom. Through tear-stained eyes and through sun-scorched lips he cried, "Remember me" (vs. 42). He did not say, "Get me off the cross"; he knew that he deserved his punishment. He did not say, "Let me live"; he knew that he deserved to die.

In the Steps of the Master

He just said, "Remember me."

Jesus did not respond by saying, "If you are good enough, I will," because He knew that no man is that good. Jesus did not say, "If you can get yourself off that old cross, I will," because He knew that no man can rescue himself. Jesus did not say, "Tomorrow," or, "Later," because there would be no tomorrow for this criminal. But with eyes of love, He looked his way; through lips of mercy, He said, "To day shalt thou be with me in paradise." Our Lord went to Calvary to bleed and die for sinners. Even while He was dying, He paused long enough to snatch another soul from the burning flames of a Devil's Hell and deliver him so he would have a place in Paradise.

That morning this poor soul was bleeding and hanging on a cross, one step away from stepping off into Hell. The next morning, he was walking down the halls of Paradise, shaking hands with Abraham, Isaac and Jacob. He was delivered with the rest of the saints when Jesus delivered up Paradise to the Third Heaven.

All humanity stands guilty and condemned before the law of God. All men are on the cross of rebellion and are just one breath away from stepping into Hell, lost forever. But, thank God, Jesus took our place; if we will realize our condition and call on Him for mercy, He will say unto us, 'Thou shalt be with Me in Paradise.' I am glad that he is the Forgiver of sinners!

In this study, one sinner was in a hogpen, another was up a tree, and the thief was on the cross. But Jesus is able to save to the uttermost and from the "guttermost." In the words of the popular gospel song, "But the greatest of all miracles was when my Jesus saved me. Yes, I know what Jesus did for me."

12

Subject: The Final Hours of Jesus Christ

Text: John 13; 18; 19; Luke 22

I. At the Table: The Upper Room—A Special Hour (John 13:14)
   A. The Table of Fellowship (vs. 2)
   B. The Towel of Humility (vss. 4–15)
   C. The Testimony of Love (vss. 34, 35)

II. In the Garden: Gethsemane—A Sorrowful Hour (Luke 22:39–46)
   A. His Approach (vs. 41)
   B. His Appeal (vs. 42)
   C. His Angels (vs. 43)
   D. His Agony (vs. 44)

III. Before the Crowd: Pilate's Hall—A Shameful Hour (John 18:25–19:16)
   A. The Release of the Criminal (18:39, 40)
   B. The Ridicule of the Company (19:1–3)
   C. The Rejection of the Christ (19:4–16)

IV. On the Cross: Calvary—A Suffering Hour (John 19:16–30)
   A. The Cross (vs. 17)
   B. The Crucifixion (vs. 18)
   C. The Cries (vss. 26–30)
   D. The Completion (vss. 31–37)

The Final Hours of Jesus Christ

As we approach this chapter, our hearts are made humble, tears fill our eyes, and we feel as if we should take off our shoes, because the ground on which we are standing is holy ground. We are entering into the passion ministry of our Lord. These are the last few hours that He spent on this earth before going to the cross and paying the sin debt for lost humanity.

Jesus told His disciples in the Upper Room that His "hour" had come. Oh, what an hour this was! This was a holy hour, an hour that had been coming since the Garden of Eden when God told the serpent that the Seed of the woman would bruise his head (Gen. 3:15). This hour had been foretold by the prophets throughout the Old Testament and had been anticipated by the Old Testament saints. This was the hour for which Jesus was born.

There has never been an hour that has changed more lives than this hour, for redemption was purchased in this hour. The demands of a holy God were met in this hour. Holy love was displayed in this hour. Sin and Satan were defeated in this hour. In this hour, a fountain was opened for sin, for the Lamb of God had come to take away the sin of the world (John 1:29). In

89

this chapter, we will look at four places where Jesus spent this hour, what kind of hour it was and what it means to us today.

The first place we see our Lord in this hour is in the Upper Room. The Feast of the Passover was drawing nigh. The Passover was a time when the Jews celebrated and commemorated the victory that God had wrought in Egypt over Pharaoh by the blood of the passover lamb. God said, "When I see the blood, I will pass over you" (Exod. 12:13). Every year since that day, the Jews were to hold the Feast of the Passover.

Jesus was with His disciples at the table in the Upper Room; on the table were roasted lamb, unleavened bread and bitter herbs. There were also a bowl of water and a cup of the fruit of the vine. It was at this table that Jesus prepared His own for His departure out of this world. He warned them of the betrayer; He spoke of His death; He even told Peter that before the cock crowed, Peter would deny Him three times. Their hearts were sad, and there were many questions in their minds, so Jesus, at the Passover table, suggested that they fellowship and break bread together one more time. He told them that they would not celebrate this feast together again until they were in His Father's kingdom. Here Jesus instituted the Lord's Supper and said, "This do in remembrance of me" (Luke 22:19). Nothing can settle the fear in our hearts like breaking bread with Jesus at the table of fellowship.

It was a custom in that day for a servant to wash the feet of important guests in one's home. Here is the King of Glory, the Holy Son of God, taking a towel and getting on His knees to wash the feet of His servants. He loved them so much that He humbled Himself and came to where they were to rescue them out of the snare of sin and to redeem their souls to God.

The bread was a type of His broken body, the fruit of the vine was a type of His shed blood, and this foot washing pointed to Calvary. There Jesus would wash not only their feet with water, but also their souls, hearts and lives with His blood. At the end of this special hour, Jesus told them to love one another, for "by this shall all men know that ye are my disciples" (John 13:35). Then they sang a hymn and went out to the Mount of Olives.

The second place we see our Lord is in the Garden of Gethsemane. This was a place where Jesus often prayed. It was a garden surrounded by a fence with a gate. Inside were eight olive trees under which Jesus knelt and prayed. This night His heart was heavy with the sin of the whole world upon Him. He was on His way to the cross and needed a special touch from His Heavenly Father. What a wonderful picture of prayer we see in this garden. Jesus was alone, and He prayed willingly and earnestly.

Nowhere in the Bible can we see the relationship between Jesus and the Father any more vividly portrayed than in this garden. Jesus cried from the depths of His soul, "Abba, Father" (Mark 14:36). "Father" is a general term, but "Abba" is deeply personal and intimate. Slaves were forbidden to use this term when addressing the head of the family. Note how W. E. Vine explains this term:

> "Abba" is the word framed by the lips of infants and betokens unreasoning trust; "Father" expresses an intelligent apprehension of the relationship. The two words together express the love and intelligent confidence of the child.

Only a child in the family could say "Abba." It is like

91

our word *papa.* When we approach God in prayer, we need to realize that He is our Father and also our Abba Father, "Papa." The Father cares what is in the heart of the son.

In this garden, Jesus had to drink of the cup filled with the sins of the whole world—past, present and future. He who knew no sin had to become sin for us, drinking of the cup of sin and God's wrath so that we might drink from the cup of salvation. His appeal was that it might pass from Him if it were possible, but He prayed for God's will above His own. I am glad that He was willing to drink from this bitter cup and that He drank every drop.

Oh, the agony of the Son of God that night in the garden! He poured out His soul unto the Father until His sweat was like great drops of blood falling down to the ground. This was a sorrowful hour. Jesus said to His disciples, "My soul is exceeding sorrowful, even unto death" (Matt. 26:38). He was a Man dying so that the lost world might be found and never die. He unselfishly gave His life a ransom for many.

The disciples were asleep, and the Roman soldiers were coming with the betrayer. All the sin of the whole human race was upon our Lord, and He was kneeling on the ground with blood, sweat and tears running down His face. His strength was about gone from his tired body. His soul was heavy and tormented by the demons of Hell, but His Father answered His prayer. He did not remove His cup, but He gave Him grace, favor and strength to bear it. God sent His mighty angels, the same angels that had announced His birth and had praised Him in eternity past. The angels that had touched Elijah, Daniel and Jesus Himself after His battle with the Devil in the wilderness of temptation came on the scene and ministered to our blessed Lord. They gave Him the power to go on in the face of agony that literally brought bloody sweat from the praying Saviour.

This is how prayer works in our lives today. If we will pray earnestly and willingly, God may not remove our burdens, but He will give us grace to go on. Before He went to His cross, He found a place of prayer. Before we can bear our cross, we must have a Gethsemane experience in our lives.

As Jesus arose from prayer and began to leave the garden, there came the flickering of the lighted torch and the scuffling of soldiers' feet. They were coming to arrest our blessed Lord. As Judas betrayed Jesus with a kiss, the guards laid hold on Him and led Him away to be tried.

The third place we see Jesus in this hour is at His trial, which was in four stages. The first two were His Jewish trial, while the second two were His Roman trial. When Jesus was led away from the garden, He was taken to the house of Annas. He was the father-in-law to the high priest of that year, a man by the name of Caiaphas. No one really knows why they brought Him there first unless it was to find something with which they could charge Him.

After His trial before Annas, they led Him to His second Jewish trial, the one before Caiaphas. This is where our Lord stood all night long while the Jewish leaders tried to come up with an accusation they could lay to His charge so that He would be worthy of death. All night long He stood and heard the charges and the slander of these wicked men. Even though these men could judge Him with their Jewish law, they did not have the authority to try capital crimes; they could not sentence Him to death. So when the morning came, they led Him away to be tried by the Roman governor, Pilate.

His Roman trial was before two men, Pilate and Herod. They brought Him first to Pilate, but he did not want anything to do with Jesus. When he heard that He was a Galilean, he sent Him to Herod, who was in the city for the Passover feast. Herod was glad to see Jesus. He had heard about Him for a long time and wanted to see one of His miracles, but Jesus would not answer him a word. The chief priests and the scribes stood and vigorously accused our Lord. Herod and his guards mocked Jesus and put on Him a purple robe and sent Him back to Pilate. So they led Jesus to the judgment hall.

They came to the place of the "pavement," where Pilate sat on the judgment seat and passed the death sentence on Jesus. "I find no fault in him," Pilate said (John 19:6), but they wanted Him dead. They cried out, "Crucify him." Pilate was set on releasing Jesus, but the Jewish leaders told him that he was not Caesar's friend if he did. So for his fear of losing his position in politics, Pilate turned Jesus over to the Jews. He knew that he could release a prisoner on the Passover, but they wanted the murderer named Barabbas rather than Jesus.

So Pilate washed his hands in water and sent Jesus to the soldiers to be beaten. Many people today are like Pilate. They will not do what is right because they are more concerned with selfish goals and with pleasing the crowd than with what they do with Jesus. Pilate found out something that this world will find out someday—water will not wash one's sins or guilt away.

Tradition says that later Pilate lived in the city of Vienne in France and that he eventually committed suicide. Only the blood of the Lamb that he put to death can take away sin and guilt.

The company of soldiers made a mock crown out of thorns and pretended to honor Jesus as a king. They then beat on Him with their hands. This was one of the most shameful hours this world has ever known.

Pilate then released Jesus to the Jews to be led away to His death. When the death sentence was passed on our Lord, the Bible says that they "led him away. And he bearing his cross went forth into a place called the place of a skull, which is called in the Hebrew Golgotha" (John 19:16,17).

The fourth place we see Jesus is on His way to Calvary. What a fearful sight this must have been! Jesus had been scourged outside of the judgment hall, and the cross was laid upon His back; the howling mob followed Him, some spitting on Him, some cursing Him, and others just mocking His holy name until they came to Calvary.

Robert Boyd wrote this about crucifixion:

Victims condemned to the cross first underwent the hideous torture of the scourge, and this was immediately inflicted on Jesus. He was now seized by some soldiers nearby and, after being stripped to the waist, was bound in a stooping posture, His hands being tied behind His back to a post or a block of wood near the tribunal. The Jews had a law that no person should be given more than forty stripes save one when flogged, but the Romans had no such law, so they often scourged their victims until they bled to death. Jesus was beaten at the pleasure of the soldiers with knots of rope or plaited leather thongs which were armed at the ends with acorn-shaped drops of lead or small pointed bones. In many cases, not only was the back of the person being scourged cut open in all directions, but even the eyes, the face and the breast were torn open, and the teeth not seldom knocked out. Under the fury of the countless stripes, the victims sometimes sank amid screams, conclusive leaps and distortions into a senseless heap; sometimes died on the spot; sometimes were taken away, an unrecognizable mass of bleeding flesh, to find deliverance in death from the inflammation and fever, sickness and shame.

It was on this bleeding back that they laid the cross. When they came to the place of the skull, they drove nails into His hands and feet and fastened Him to the wooden pole. His head was crowned with thorns, His hands were nailed to a cross, and His bleeding back was rubbed up and down on the cross. Blood, sweat and tears ran down His face as the Son of God died for the sons of men, that the sons of men might become the sons of God.

He became what *we were* so that we might become what *He is.* He came to where *we were* so that we might go to where *He is.* He took our place and punishment. He died so that we might live. He cried from the cross, "I thirst," so that we might drink from the cup of salvation. He cried, "My God, my God, why hast thou forsaken me" so that we would never have to be forsaken. He cried, "Father, forgive them" so that we might have forgiveness through His blood. He cried to His foes. He cried out to His mother.

He cried out to His God, "It is finished"; and God the Father heard his cry, accepted His sacrifice and answered His prayer. As God the Father dropped the veil of darkness over the cross of Calvary, Jesus Christ His Son paid the sin debt for every man.

The Final Hours of Jesus Christ

Alas! And did my Saviour bleed?
And did my Sovereign die?
Would He devote that sacred head
For such a worm as I?

—Isaac Watts

13

Subject: The Resurrection of Jesus Christ

Text: John 20:1–18

I. Predicted by the Scriptures

    A. The Types Foreshadowing It

    B. The Truths Foretelling It

II. Proclaimed by the Saviour

    A. By His Marvelous Words

    B. By His Miraculous Works

III. Performed by the Spirit

    A. The Spirit and His Virgin Birth

    B. The Spirit and His Vital Ministry

    C. The Spirit and His Victorious Resurrection

IV. Preached by the Saints

    A. By Peter in Jerusalem

    B. By Philip in the Desert

    C. By Paul in Athens

V. Promised to the Saved

    A. A Perfect Promise

In the Steps of the Master

    B. A Personal Promise
    C. A Precious Promise

The Resurrection of Jesus Christ

We come now to the greatest event in the life of our Lord: His resurrection from the dead. The earthly life of Jesus was surrounded by miracles. His conception in the virgin womb of Mary was a miracle, and now at the close of His earthly life, we see a miracle just as great as His birth—He arose! In fact, all of the other miracles are validated by His resurrection. If Christ had not risen, his preaching, miracles and death on the cross would have been in vain. It was of utmost importance that He conquer death, Hell and the grave. All this He did in His resurrection.

The resurrection of Christ was not an afterthought with God. Just like His death, it was planned by God before the foundation of the world. Even the Old Testament contains types and foreshadowings of His resurrection. When Abraham offered up his son Isaac on the altar, he told the men who went with them, "Abide ye here with the ass; and I and the lad will go yonder and worship, and come again to you." (Gen. 22:5). Abraham believed with all his heart that if Isaac died on that mountain, God would raise him from the dead (Heb. 11:19).

Joseph is also a type of Christ (Gen. 37). He was hated by his own brethren and was put into a pit. His brothers sat and ate as if nothing had happened. This is what the Jews did to our blessed Lord; they nailed Him to the old rugged cross, and then they sat and watched Him die. However, God was with Joseph and brought him out of the pit safe and sound. Jesus went down into the pit of death, but God was faithful and raised Him up and loosed Him from the pangs of death.

In Leviticus 14, the two birds that were used in the sacrifice for the cleansing of the leper also typify Christ. These two birds represent the two natures of Christ—His humanity and His deity. One bird was killed, and the other bird, along with some hyssop, was dipped in his blood. The leper was sprinkled with blood seven times, and the living bird was released. The dead bird is a type of the death of Christ, while the living bird is a type of the resurrection of Christ. I can almost hear the little bird, as he flies away, singing the hymn by Fanny Crosby, "Redeemed, redeemed, redeemed by the blood of the Lamb."

The resurrection is seen in the Old Testament, not only in type, but also in truth. It was not only fore-shadowed, but it was also foretold. It was not only pictured, but it was also predicted. In Psalm 16, David, under the inspiration of the Holy Spirit, looked beyond his sorrow and distress and said concerning Christ, "For thou wilt not leave my soul in hell; neither wilt thou suffer thine Holy One to see corruption." Truly, this is a psalm of resurrection.

Seven hundred years before the birth of Jesus, Isaiah had a vision of the Redeemer. He saw His sorrow and suffering; he saw His sinless life and His substitutionary death; but, thank God, he also saw His supernatural resurrection. Through the telescope of divine revelation, Isaiah said, "He shall see his seed, he shall prolong his days, and the pleasure of the Lord shall prosper in his hand" (53:10).

The apostle Paul in his letter to the church at Corinth said that Christ died and was buried and was raised again "according to the scriptures" (I Cor. 15:3, 4). The resurrection of our Lord was revealed without dispute in the Old Testament. Even Job in his distress said, "I know that my redeemer liveth" (19:25).

The great truth of the resurrection was proclaimed by Jesus Himself. When Jesus said, "Destroy this temple, and in three days I will raise it up" (John 2:19), He was not talking about the temple that took the Jews forty-six years to build. Rather, He spoke of the temple of His body—the one not made with earthly hands.

In Matthew 12, Jesus gave the Pharisees the sign of the prophet Jonah. Jesus said, "As Jonas was three days and three nights in the whale's belly; so shall the Son of man be three days and three nights in the heart of the earth." Jonah is an Old Testament picture of our buried and risen Saviour. Jesus said that one "greater than Jonas is here" (vss. 40, 41).

On the road to Calvary, Jesus told His disciples, "Ye now therefore have sorrow: but I will see you again" (John 16:22).

Jesus proclaimed His resurrection not only in the messages that He preached, but also in the miracles that He performed. In Luke 7, when Jesus raised up the only son of the widow woman, He was proclaiming His resurrection. In Mark 5, when Jesus raised up the daughter of Jairus, He was proclaiming His resurrection. When He raised up Lazarus from the dead after he had been dead four days, He was proclaiming His resurrection. Jesus said to the crowd that happy day, "I am the resurrection, and the life" (John 11:25). He knew from the beginning that He would rise again.

The resurrection of Jesus was performed by the Holy Spirit. The Bible says in Romans 8:11, "But if the Spirit of him that raised up Jesus from the dead dwell in you, he that raised up Christ from the dead shall also quicken your mortal bodies by his Spirit that dwelleth in you." Yes, Jesus was raised up from the dead by the power of the Holy Spirit. It was the Holy Spirit that conceived the Christ child in the virgin womb of Mary. It was the Holy Spirit that anointed Jesus to preach the Gospel and sent Him to bind up the brokenhearted, to proclaim liberty to the captives and to open the prison to them that are bound. It was also the Holy Spirit that quickened the dead body of Jesus.

I can hear the Roman soldiers as they say, "We've got Him now." I can see the worried looks on the faces of His disciples as they thought that their Lord was forever gone. But let us go to the tomb in the early morning hours on the first day of the week after His crucifixion. As we stand there, we can see the skin begin to loosen on His face. We can see His eyelids begin to twitch. We watch as His chest begins to heave. We stand in awe as the breath of God flows through His body:

> Up from the grave He arose,
> With a mighty triumph o'er His foes;
> He arose a Victor from the dark domain,
> And He lives forever with His saints to reign.
> He arose! He arose! Hallelujah! Christ arose!

> —Robert Lowry

Christ's resurrection was the theme of the message of the apostles in the days of the early church. Peter, on the day of Pentecost, filled with the Holy Ghost, stood in the midst of the people and preached Jesus crucified, buried and *risen*. Peter proclaimed, "God hath raised [Him] up, having loosed the pains of death: because it was not possible that he should be holden of it" (Acts 2:24).

When the Holy Ghost led Philip into the desert to preach to one man, he found the eunuch reading from Isaiah 53. The Ethiopian told Philip that he needed some man to guide him so that he might understand what he was reading. Philip got into the chariot and "began at the same scripture, and preached unto him Jesus" (Acts 8:35). One cannot preach Jesus and not deal with the resurrection. If Christ had not risen, He would not be the holy, pure and true Son of God. Our preaching today ought to lift up and magnify the death, burial and resurrection of Jesus.

When the apostle Paul stood on top of Mars' hill, he said to those who through idolatry were bound by spiritual ignorance that God "hath appointed a day, in the which he will judge the world in righteousness by that man whom he hath ordained; whereof he hath given assurance unto all men, in that he hath raised him from the dead" (Acts 17:31).

In I Corinthians 15:19, Paul, under the inspiration of the Holy Spirit, says, "If in this life only we have hope in Christ, we are of all men most miserable." Why? Why would we be miserable? Because if Christ be not risen, there would be no resurrection of the dead. There would be no life beyond this vale of tears. We would not have the hope that we will see our loved ones again. If Christ be not risen, our hope, our faith, even our preaching would be totally in vain. But, thank God, because He lives, we too shall live. Christ's resurrection assures and guarantees our resurrection.

In John 14:19, our Lord made us a promise. He said, "Because I live, ye shall live also." Our resurrection is based on the fact that *He lives!* This is a perfect promise given to His own. Those who receive Him as their Saviour will live again. This is a personal promise. Oh, how precious is the promise that we will live again and see our loved ones again.

Many years ago, Job, sitting in the ash heap, lifted up his voice and shouted,

> *"I know that my redeemer liveth, and that he shall stand at the latter day upon the earth:*
> *"And though after my skin worms destroy this body, yet in my flesh shall I see God."*—19:25, 26.

Death is *not* the end. There is hope beyond the grave. Our Lord Jesus has taken away the sting of death and has robbed the grave of its victory. So often I have found comfort in the words of the popular song,

> Because He lives, I can face tomorrow;
> Because He lives, all fear is gone.
> Because I know He holds the future,
> Life is worth the living just
> BECAUSE HE LIVES!

14

Subject: The Ascension of Jesus Christ

Text: Acts 1:1–11

I. The Proof of His Resurrection (vs. 3)
   A. The Resurrected Saints (Open Graves)
   B. The Revived Saints (Emmaus Road)
   C. The Rejoicing Saints (Upper Room)

II. The Preparation of His Redeemed (vss. 3–8)
   A. Collected (vs. 4)
   B. Commanded (vs. 4)
   C. Commissioned (vs. 8)
      1. The Waiting on His Power
      2. The Witness of His Person
      3. The Working of His Plan

III. The Picture of His Royalty (vss. 9, 10)
   A. Robbing of the Grave
   B. Reversal of Gravity
   C. Reception Into Glory
      1. The Cloud
      2. The Company
      3. The Course (Back to the Father)

IV. The Purpose of His Rapture
   A. To Send the Holy Spirit
   B. To Sit Down at the Father's Right Hand
   C. To Secure Our Standing With the Father

In the Steps of the Master

V. The Promise of His Return (vs. 11)
   A. The Person: "this same Jesus"
   B. The Prediction: "shall so come"
   C. The Pattern: "in like manner"

The Ascension of Jesus Christ

We come now to the last scene in the earthly life of Jesus Christ: His ascension. He told His disciples that He would go back to the Father, and now He is going. Let us look at some things that happened *before* His ascension, some truths that were revealed *during* His ascension and some thrills that took place *after* His ascension and see what they mean to us today.

Before Jesus went back to Heaven, He infallibly proved that He had risen from the dead. Note just three places where Jesus proved His power over death and showed Himself alive.

Matthew 27:52, 53 say,

> "And the graves were opened; and many bodies of the saints which slept arose,
>
> "And came out of the graves after his resurrection, and went into the holy city, and appeared unto many."

This was just a little foretaste of the great resurrection day of the saints. If He had not risen, they would not rise.

Luke 24 tells of two followers of Jesus on the road to Emmaus. While they talked and communed together, Jesus drew near. They did not know at first that it was

Jesus. He started with Moses and went down through the prophets and opened their eyes to those things concerning Himself. When Jesus went in to break bread with them, He blessed and broke it, and they knew that He was Jesus. He then vanished out of their sight. When He was gone, they said one to another, "Did not our heart burn within us, while he talked with us by the way?" (vs. 32). He proved to these disciples that He was alive, and He touched their hearts with His burning presence. The *thought* of Him ought to cause "holy heartburn."

There was joy in the Upper Room where the disciples were gathered. Jesus stood in the midst and spoke peace to their souls. The Bible says, "Then were the disciples glad, when they saw the Lord" (John 20:20).

Before Jesus went back to His Father, He had to prepare His people for His leaving. He did not want to leave them scattered and afraid. First, there was Mary, who was weeping; He had to dry her tears and let her know that He was alive and well. Next, was doubting Thomas; the Lord had to show Himself to him and settle the doubt in his mind and heart. Then there was Peter. He had cursed and openly denied his Lord; he was out weeping bitterly, so Jesus had to let him know that He still loved him and had a great plan for his life. He wanted Peter to know that failure was not final.

Jesus, before He went Home, had to give His servants His last will or His plan for their lives. He commanded them to wait for the power of the Holy Ghost, and He commissioned them to be witnesses for Him unto the uttermost parts of the earth (Acts 1:8).

In the ascension of our Lord, we have a picture of His royalty. This was no ordinary man. He was different; He was unique; He was the King of Glory. Let us notice three ways His royalty is pictured.

First, He robbed the grave. No one from Adam to John the Baptist had ever gotten up from the grave by his own power. The grave had been very successful in holding its victims. But death could not *hold* Him. Hell did not *want* Him, and the grave could not *keep* Him. Other kings have lived and died; they are still in their graves. But King Jesus lives. The grave has been robbed, and His tomb is empty today.

Second, He reversed gravity. Gravity is that unseen power which draws all people and things to the earth. Everything is bound to this earth by gravity. The law of gravity tells us that what goes up must come down. But when Christ was taken up, He reversed gravity. He was the only one who went up. God turned off gravity just on the spot where Jesus stood.

Third, He was received up into Glory. This was the day when Jesus went Home. In the Old Testament, the cloud was a symbol of the presence of God. God led the children of Israel through the wilderness by a cloud. So God came down in a cloud and wrapped Himself around Jesus and lifted Him back to Heaven where He was welcomed by companies of angels

This was the joy that was set before Him. Like the general of an army that had been sent to defeat a foe, His mission was now complete. The victory had been won, and now He was going Home where a hero's welcome awaited Him. He was going back to the Father from whom He came.

One might ask, "Why did Jesus go back to Heaven?

In the Steps of the Master

Why did He not stay after His resurrection?" To answer this question, let us notice three reasons Jesus went back to Heaven.

First, He went back to send the Holy Spirit. Jesus said in John 16:7, "Nevertheless I tell you the truth; It is expedient for you that I go away: for if I go not away, the Comforter will not come unto you; but if I depart, I will send him unto you." Ten days after His ascension, on the day of Pentecost, He kept this promise, and the Holy Spirit came. Jesus is here today in the Person of the Holy Spirit.

Second, He went away to sit down at the right hand of the Father. This shows that His work was completely finished. David, under the inspiration of the Holy Spirit, prophesied in Psalm 110:1: "The LORD said unto my Lord, Sit thou at my right hand, until I make thine enemies thy footstool." The high priest in the Old Testament could never sit down in the Holy of Holies because his work was never done. But our Lord finished the job, went back Home victorious and sat down in the seat of authority at the Father's right hand.

Third, He went back to be our Great High Priest. He is our Advocate with the Father. He is there pleading our case and making intercession for the saints of God. When the Devil tries to bring up our past and present our faults, Jesus is there to be our Lawyer. He just points to the blood He shed, and the Father says, "Case dismissed!" I am so glad that He went back to secure our standing with the Father. That is why the song-writer Robert C. Loveless said,

> Jesus saves and keeps me,
> And He's the one I'm waiting for.
> Every day with Jesus
> Is sweeter than the day before.

Acts 1:11 gives us the promise of His return. He went away, but not for long; He will return!

Notice the Person: "this same Jesus." This is the One who was born of a virgin; the One who lived a sinless life; the One who healed the sick, fed the hungry and raised the dead; the One who went to Calvary and shed His blood for our sins; the One who got up from the grave and the One who ever liveth to make intercession for the saints of God. *This same* Jesus—not a prophet, not an angel, not Moses or Jacob or Paul—but the Lord Jesus Christ Himself!

Notice the prediction: "shall so come." This is not a hope-so or a maybe-so promise. "He that shall come *will come,* and *will not tarry*" (Heb. 10:37). There are some things of which I am not sure, but this one thing I know: He will come again. This hope is anchored deep in the heart of my soul. Jesus Himself made the sure promise, "If I go...*I will come again*" (John 14:3).

Notice the pattern: "in like manner." Just like He went away, so He will come again. He went away in a body, and He will return in a body. He went away in a cloud, and He will return in a cloud. They saw Him go up, and there will be those who will see Him come down.

The next time He comes, they will not spit on Him and cry, "Crucify Him!" They will not nail Him to a cross. The next time He comes, He will not come as a Baby in a manger, but He will come as King of Kings and Lord of Lords. Yes, He went away, but not to stay; He is coming back again.

MARANATHA! OUR LORD IS COMING!

At the close of our study, let us notice a soul-stirring excerpt from Alfred Edersheim's book entitled *The Life and Times of Jesus the Messiah:*

Amen! It is so. Ring out the bells of Heaven; sing forth the angelic welcome of worship; carry it to the utmost bounds of the earth! Shine forth from Bethany, Thou Sun of Righteousness, and chase away earth's mist and darkness, for Heaven's golden day has broken.

Conclusion

From His birth to His ascension, we have followed the Master. We have heard His words, we have seen His miracles, we have felt His own tender touch upon our souls, and now may our daily lives show to others that we have been with Jesus. Our eyes have been made to see Him, our hearts have been made to love Him, and now may our lives be made to follow His example.

I Peter 2:21 says, "For even hereunto were ye called: because Christ also suffered for us, leaving us an example, that ye should *follow* his steps." Let us follow the way He prayed. Let us follow the way He loved sinners and helped the needy. Let us follow His holy character. May His image be stamped upon our lives.

THE WORLD ITSELF COULD NOT CONTAIN THE BOOKS!

John the Beloved said that if everything Jesus did was written in a book, "the world itself could not contain the books that should be written" (vss. 21:25).

In these writings, I am well aware that I have not touched the hem of His garments. Half of the half has not been told in this volume. But it is my prayer that as we have followed our Lord, your heart has been stirred anew, and that you have found some fresh material that will enhance your preaching on the life of our Lord.

Twenty-Five Glorious Pictures of Jesus in the Gospel of John

Chapter 1—He is the Sin Taker

Chapter 2—He is the Wine Maker

Chapter 3—He is the Love Giver

Chapter 4—He is the Soul Satisfier

Chapter 5—He is the Sick Healer

Chapter 6—He is the Bread Breaker and the Wave Walker

Chapter 7—He is the Thirst Quencher

Chapter 8—He is the Life Changer

Chapter 9—He is the Eye Opener

Chapter 10—He is the Sheep Keeper

Chapter 11—He is the Dead Raiser

Chapter 12—He is the Light Shiner

Chapter 13—He is the Foot Washer

Chapter 14—He is the Heart Calmer and the Mansion Builder

Chapter 15—He is the Branch Purger

Chapter 16—He is the Spirit Sender

Chapter 17—He is the Prayer Pray-er

Chapter 18—He is the Cup Drinker

Chapter 19—He is the Cross Bearer and the Blood Shedder

Chapter 20—He is the Grave Robber and the Peace Speaker

Chapter 21—He is the Table Spreader

For a complete list of available books, write to:
Sword of the Lord Publishers
P.O. Box 1099
Murfreesboro, Tennessee 37133.

(800) 24-SWORD
FAX (615) 278-1309
www.swordofthelord.com